AROUND THE WORLD
WITH NO HASSLES

A Travel Journal

TIVERTON PRESS

WESTPORT, CONNECTICUT

Tiverton Press
15 Ferry Lane East
Westport, CT 06880-6041

Around the World With No Hassles
a Travel Journal

1991

All photographs are by the author

Grateful acknowledgement is made for
permission to reprint the excerpt
from *Diana's Diary, An Intimate Portrait
of the Princess of Wales,*
by Andrew Norton. Reprinted with
permission of Summit Books.

Library of Congress
Catalogue Card #91-091246
ISBN 0-9603578-1-5
Printed in the United States of America

Type conversion, output to film, printing and binding
The J. S. McCarthy Company, Offset Printers
Augusta, Maine

For Lynn

Without whom—nothing

Whose love and wisdom

Have informed my life always.

With many thanks to those who have been interested and who have cared and helped, especially Tufan Cankat, Linda Duval, Lynn Frost, Emily McConnell, Lucretia McDine, Jerry Morris, Campbell Niven, Sioux Paxton, Rhoda Truax Silberman, Kathy Vary and Paul Woelfel.

TABLE OF CONTENTS

AROUND THE WORLD
WITH NO HASSLES

Being the record of a journey which took us
115 days and involved two backpacks, one
camera and one typewriter.

INTRODUCTION

To go around the world! To see exotic places
we had never even hoped to see! To visit friends in
faraway places! Yes! This had long been the stuff
to dream on.

"But, whoa!" said our heads. "What about
obligations? What about the time lost? What about
the cost?"

"Go now!" said our hearts. "Do not wait!"

Maybe all of life is a conflict between the
head and the heart. Maybe our hearts are an under-
represented minority. Maybe our heads, always so
logical and serious, need to be removed (from
control) now and then.

Early in 1989, when the days were short and
the nights were long and cold, Lynn and I began to
listen carefully to our hearts. By the end of March
we knew that our trip would become a reality.

We notified family and friends, and we began
to write letters to those who might just say, "Come
by and see us." The responses were exciting.

In fact, we built our trip around specific dates
and specific places. As we went along, the plot
thickened and the web tightened. The grand scheme
became more and more definite as spring advanced.

Critically important to our planning was the invitation that had got our dream started. This had come from our friends Richard and Penny Post who had moved to Hong Kong. "Do come and visit us," were Penny's incautious last words as they left Connecticut. Since the Posts travel a lot, we arranged from the start to schedule our time in Hong Kong very precisely. Their schedule and ours had to mesh.

"If you are going to do the Nile, you must book a tour," said our ever-wise travel agent and counselor, Fritz Riegel, through whose travel agency, The Travel Bureau, Inc., in Wilton, Connecticut, we made all our arrangements. The Nile tour, once set up, gave us another time period to plan around.

Each time an engagement became firm or an invitation became definite, we were more and more drawn into a schedule that lost its flexibility. All this led finally to the actual booking of flights, a procedure that locked us into beginning and ending dates in each country we visited.

We also booked ourselves into hotels at most destinations so that for the first night, at least, in a new country, we would know exactly where we were going and where we would stay.

By the middle of July, our plan was complete, and our journey had firm and definite outlines. First we would spend three days in the west of Ireland, and then three days in Dublin; and last, we would fly back from Tahiti and be home again at the beginning of the new year.

Thus it was that Lynn and I got ready for our long trip, the first of such scope in our lifetime. We found that the experience was exhilarating and rewarding in untold numbers of ways. As time wore on, we became travel wise.

We learned that our son Bill was right when he warned us that a day of travel is a day out of your trip. We learned to pace ourselves. Sightseeing is fun, but there need to be days of relief from any kind of pace at all.

Several friends had advised us to take only one bag apiece and to make that a backpack. We learned that the wisdom of that decision benefited us constantly. Having our hands free was extremely valuable always, and carrying our own luggage onto planes meant that we never lost anything and we were never delayed by waiting for baggage.

We had never traveled to any great extent and we got a taste of what some world travelers know all about. It's a heady experience to be out there, away from "real life" and answerable to no one. We loved it. But when the time came to get back to our home, we found that we were ready for that, too.

What follows derives from the journal that I kept on the trip. Some parts of this book have appeared before in newspapers. Some of what follows was written after our return.

IRELAND

A savant once said that "there are as many Hamlets as there have been actors who have played the role." I've always loved the great truth in that statement. A role is not a strait jacket for an actor. It is, rather, a tool which the artist can use, much in the way a painter uses his palette and brushes, to express himself.

And it is also true that there is not just one Ireland. There are endless numbers of Irelands, and it is up to the traveler to find the one that he will enjoy most. Travel, at its best and most enjoyable, should be a voyage of discovery. There is no "must do" or "must see" on a good vacation trip, and one of the most rewarding kinds of adventuring is to leave behind all the sage advice so urgently given by well-wishers, and head off for unknown territories.

The west of Ireland has always had a special pull for me ever since I read and then directed a production of John Millington Synge's play, "The Playboy of the Western World." The action in this play is set in the west country, and the language he uses in it expresses the rich and special qualities of the speech of the people here. In my production of this great play, I was lucky enough to have cast Westport's now busy model and actress, Topher Barrett, as Pegeen Mike.

And so, now in Ireland, Lynn and I decided to take a look at some of the wonders of the west. We didn't ignore Galway and Galway Bay, and we did see the remarkably thrilling sunset that is so fabled. But beyond Galway lies Connemara with its moonscape desolation, high barren mountains and rock-strewn, tiny grazing fields which seem to support a remarkable number of black-faced, well-rounded sheep.

We spent our first night in Ireland at the Cashel House Hotel, a quietly elegant country house set on 35 acres of coastal land, overlooking lovely, wild Cashel Bay, and crowded with a rich variety of flowering shrubs and flowers.

As we traveled, the Irish punt was worth about $1.40, and our large room with its handsome four-poster, many paintings, fine table for snacks or breakfast, first-rate bathroom, and so on, cost about $80 per night.

Shortly after settling into our luxurious room at Cashel House, we were surprised to hear a knock at the door. We answered, and in came a charming colleen in full maid's uniform, carrying a chilled bottle of fine champagne.

We opened the note attached to the bottle and read, "With best wishes for a happy trip." It was signed by our ever-concerned travel agent, Fritz Riegel of Wilton, Connecticut.

As we sipped the delightful nectar, we thanked Fritz quietly for arranging such a sumptuous first night in magical Ireland. Cashel House provided us with one of the most elegant experiences of our trip, and we loved it. Knowing about those special, out-of-the-way delights is one of the marks of a good travel agent. We were lucky, and we enjoyed it immensely.

At that price, we decided we would not stay long, but it was well worth it. General de Gaulle stayed here for a couple of weeks once, and it is easy to see why. The hotel's beach is tiny, but its sand is pure and sparkling white. The building is a handsome former country house, and its bright white facade stands out against the bleak mountain that rises just behind it. The chef is exceptionally talented and knows very well just what to do with the fresh salmon and fresh sea trout that abound in this fisherman's area of Ireland.

If you want to go out and catch your own, the hotel will make the arrangements for you.

More budget-oriented accommodations abound. Many are available for as little as ten punts per person per night, and of course that includes breakfast. There is a regulating agency in Ireland, and those B & Bs that display the shamrock of approval are sure to have clean rooms, fresh linen and plumbing that works.

One of the pleasures of life in general, and travel in particular, is myth smashing. For example, we had heard that the roads in Ireland are terrible, and the Irish drive like madmen. "You take your life in your hands," people said. Our experience proved the opposite to be true.

Irish roads are mainly two-lane blacktops, but many have well-paved wide shoulders, and the typical Irish truck driver will pull way over when he slows down on an upgrade. Courtesy marks the driving of just about everybody, we found. The national speed limit is 50 miles per hour, and as you go into towns and villages you get into 40- and 30-mph zones. In the west there is little traffic, and as we drove around in Connemara we often went for miles without seeing another car.

We got lost at one point and asked a friendly

shopkeeper for directions It was getting late, and he suggested a shortcut through the mountains. The road barely showed on our map, but we decided to take it. And we were glad we did.

This little unmarked road was a real one-laner. At first it was paved, but that gave out, and we followed the dirt tracks with no difficulty. On either side the sod rose above the level of the road, so there was no getting off. The terrain we were going through was unpopulated. The land was covered with large rocks and sparse grass. Frequently we saw small tarns with mirrorlike surfaces reflecting the looming mountains all around us. It was sensationally beautiful.

Then we came up behind the only other piece of traffic we were to see on this road, and that was a huge tractor-trailer rig that was creeping. I shifted into a lower gear and a slower mood and let my thoughts dwell upon the lack of need for speed on a vacation. But, sure enough, the trucker shortly came to one of the rare places on this road where you can pull off, and he did so, letting us continue. We tooted and waved to thank the driver for what we were going to find over and over was his typical Irish courtesy.

From Cashel House at the head of Cashel Bay we made our way one morning to the little fishing village of Roundstone. This charmer is billed in the latest copy of *The Galway Guide* as an "artists' haven." Roundstone claims to have the longest, quietest and most golden beaches in the whole of Ireland. We saw no reason to question the truth of that claim.

The harbor was built years ago and features massive stone monuments to mark the channel, which would be lost completely at high tide since the rise and fall here is 18 feet. At low water huge masses of rock covered with seaweed give ample warning to the viewer of what might happen if he lost his way coming into the harbor even at high water.

At low tide most boats simply sit on the quite hard mud and lean against the quays, which are also enormously impressive monuments to the skill and hard work of earlier seafarers who made the harbor the beautiful place that it is.

In Gaelic the town of Roundstone is called "Cloch na Ron," which means, literally, "Rock of the Seals." Near the northern entrance to Roundstone there is a nicely situated B & B called Seal Rock B & B, and it looks out over the rock itself.

Roundstone clings to the side of a rugged mountain, and its main street rises to a height of perhaps a hundred feet and then dips down suddenly to water level. From the high point vantage we parked and walked along the main street, enjoying the view of the severely barren landscape, punctuated by tidal waters.

We were in Roundstone on a Sunday morning, and along around 11 o'clock we sensed that the sun was "over the yard arm," as they say. So, having walked from one end of the main drag to the other, we selected a small pub that looked cozy, and dropped in for a pint.

There were a few patrons, quietly enjoying the not cold beer and a pipeful. We assumed that the lady behind the bar was the owner of the establishment, and she greeted us cordially. After a couple of words had been said, we were asked, in the friendliest way, "And where are you from, then?"

Gradually, our multi-faceted origins poured out across the bar, and when our hostess heard the word Boston, she cheerfully said, "Take a look behind you!"

There on the wall behind us, framed nicely in a slim, dark wooden frame, was a dish towel dedicated in its design to the Boston Tea Party and American Liberty. We began to feel quite at home as we learned about our hostess's family in the States. We also realized anew that America has a special place in the hearts of the Irish, because of the fact that we kicked out the British so many years ago. It's a special bond, for sure.

We emerged from this charming little "snug" just as the morning church service ended and the streets filled with families in fine garb enjoying the bright warmth of a lovely sunny morning. At the candy stores, little nippers lined up to get their penny-dreadfuls, payment we assumed for having kept their mouths shut in church.

We climbed back up the hill to its peak in front of the quietly elegant Roundstone Hotel, and sat in our car to eat the sandwich we had put together from last night's dinner's leftovers.

We were constantly delighted by the stone walls that are everywhere in much of Connemara. The walls were built to keep livestock in, and they define tiny fields. Here and there thatch-roofed cottages, also built of stone, persevere ruggedly. Many are abandoned, and some have new, non-thatch roofs.

In total contrast to the roughness of the landscape in the west of Ireland, is the ready warmth and friendliness of the people who live there. Lynn and I were welcomed into the lives of the folks we stopped to talk to whenever that happened, and it is easy to strike up a conversation with these people.

We found that Ireland is truly the land of "a hundred thousand welcomes." Or as they say it, "Cead Mile Failte!"

* * *

On the way back from the west of Ireland we went through the small city of Athlone, and we spent the night there. Athlone is on the west bank of the River Shannon, at this point running from north to south. As you enter the city, you come up to the huge castle at the edge of the river. We parked in the center of a three-way intersection there right next to the Tourist Information Office.

The Office gave us information about the city, and they booked us into a B & B. After a bit of sightseeing, we easily located our lodgings and were delighted to find that it was clean, neat and in every way a first-class little hotel. The night's stay cost about $30 and included a generous and tasty breakfast.

Athlone is located at the place where the River Shannon was easiest to ford. Upstream the river is very wide, and downstream it is deep and also often wide. The shallow rapids at this location made it easy in the old days for the forces from Meath to the east to attack the West Meath folks; hence, over the years a defensive fortress was built. The present fortress was started in the twelfth century and improved over the years. It still looks pretty impenetrable.

In the middle of the 19th century, the canal building urge swept over Europe, and a dam was built at Athlone and locks for the shipping that made the city a busy port. There is no longer any freight traffic on the River Shannon, but along the quays at the edge there are many of the old, narrow barges that have been made into houseboats.

Observing the action at the lock is interesting. There was a high wind the day I watched, and the lock was busy with small motor cruisers heading up and down river, and skittering around as the wind took them. It is easy to arrange a river cruise for either a few hours, or a day, or several days. The fishing is reported to be excellent.

As we motored in Ireland, we had the radio on often in our car, and we were amused by a talk show host who was interviewing the mayor of a small town somewhere.

"Well, Mr. Mayor," the host said, "and are you pleased that your little town has finally won the National Tidy Town Award?"

"Oh, indeed," replied the mayor. "It's a fine thing for our city."

"And isn't it true that your town was a finalist six times in a row up until this year?"

"Yes, yes, that's true," the mayor said.

"And how did that feel?"

"You know," the mayor said reflectively, "it was sort of like always a bridesmaid, never a bride!"

Cashel House gave us an elegant start in our tour of otherwise quite wild Connemara. We loved it!

We ascended to the very top where "stately plump Buck Mulligan" made his historic entrance.

DUBLIN

The drive from Athlone to Dublin is easy and short. The two-lane road is generally good, and if you don't try to hurry, you are quite comfortable. The map that got us into Dublin was the Avis detail map. It reports that the Avis headquarters in Dublin is on Hanover Street, but oddly it does not show Hanover Street at all! However, in other ways it was a good map, and we had no trouble finding our hotel in the center of the city.

In our brief two-day stay we had specific targets, and we were able to get to them all with no difficulty. Our hotel was just off Grafton Street. If you go down Grafton Street to the River Liffey and cross it, you are then on O'Connell Street. Walking along these famous streets was one of our goals, and after crossing the Liffey we went for two blocks, turned right and shortly were at the illustrious Abbey Theatre.

The Abbey was presenting five one-act plays by Yeats which together comprise the "Cuchulain Cycle." I had read those plays years ago with interest, so I was delighted to find that we could get tickets for that evening. Our tickets were 6 pounds apiece (about $8.00), and they were good seats.

From the ticket saleslady we learned of a good restaurant nearby called the Left Bank. We had a dinner of Dublin prawns there just before the show and thus avoided that awful after-dinner, pre-theatre rush that we hate. The dinner was exceptionally good and nicely served.

The following night we saw "The Plough and the Stars" at the Gaiety Theatre. This O'Casey classic was wonderfully done and was played to a house full of enthusiastic viewers. We had dinner this night at Dan Tana's (about $35.00). This is a good wine bar and restaurant just a door or two away from the grand old Gaiety Theatre.

The National Gallery of Art in Dublin is a fine city art museum. The special show going on during our visit was a self-portrait show featuring 50 or 60 painters and sculptors. It was a great show, and we wondered why more galleries don't give that a try. Admission is free.

Who could visit Dublin and miss his chance to get to some of the locations from Joyce's "Ulysses?" Well, not us, for sure. So, dedicated as we were to the spirit of literary investigation, we set out in search of the famous Martello Tower. After all, Leopold Bloom's house at 7 Eccles Street has been torn down, and Night Town seemed not to be exactly what Lynn and I would enjoy, at least as a family outing.

Not knowing how to get to the Tower, and not finding directions in our tourist packet, we stopped in at a bookstore. Of course they would know about it.

"The what?" asked the busy clerk from the top of a ladder. "Never heard of it!" I thanked him, and we wandered on.

Finally a bus driver turned out to be the right person to ask. *He* knew where Sandy Cove is and told us to take the DART. We discovered that the DART (Dublin Area Rapid Transit) has trains about every 15 minutes to Sandy Cove, the site of the Martello Tower, scene of the opening of Joyce's major novel.

The train was cheap, fast and clean, and we were in Sandy Cove in a trice. There we had a short walk to the Tower, which is on a slight rise almost precisely at the edge of the bay to the south of Dublin, about 8 miles away.

The Martello Towers (there are several of them) were built by the British early in the 19th century to protect against possible invasion by Napoleon's forces. The invasion never came, and the towers were never used in battle. In 1904 the Tower at Sandy Cove was sold to a private buyer. The first tenant in the Tower was Oliver St. John Gogarty, a medical student, bon vivant, writer, and friend of Joyce.

Joyce only stayed in the Tower for a few days, but the experience gave him all he needed to let him start his novel with the entrance onto the top of the Tower of "stately, plump Buck Mulligan," the medical student character in the novel who is based upon the real-life Gogarty.

Now the Tower contains a good museum and a fine bookstore. There are many tributes there to such people as John Huston and Samuel Beckett, whose generosity has helped make the museum a possibility.

Below the Tower, at the water's edge, are two swimming areas. On the day we were there one was busy with swimmers of all ages. The other area, mentioned in Joyce's novel, is reserved for men. It is a well-known nude swimming area, and recently, according to usually reliable sources, it was invaded at its busiest time by a troop of young women swimmers who dared to increase the variety of the nudity in the area.

No visit to Dublin could be complete without a viewing of the Book of Kells, housed in the long room of the library at Trinity College, which was founded by Queen Elizabeth the First. As I bought my tickets, I commented to the salesgirl that the college was a result of a great Queen's gift, and her answer was, "Yes, and it was probably Irish money!"

Seriously, the great book is worth every moment spent on it. The quality of the work of illustration is truly dazzling, and the fact that the colors have kept their vibrancy despite over eleven hundred years of age and much mistreatment is something one can never forget.

When we said we were going to Dublin, a good friend gave us this ominous word of caution, "Don't forget, the streets of Dublin are dangerous," he said. I did not reply by telling him that my own brother, Steve, has been mugged twice in the past year in the streets of New York. Perhaps all city streets are dangerous these days, but I've never felt better about a city than I did about beautiful Dublin.

ENGLAND

Our decision to spend a bit more than a week in relaxed touring of the west and southwest of England was a wise one. If you need to get away from schedules, deadlines, commitments and due dates, this is a great and reasonable way to do it.

We arranged for our rental car from the U.S. because doing so gets you a good saving. And our car was ready for us only a few minutes after touchdown at Heathrow. We found that what we had was a 200 series Rover four-door sedan. It is a fine car and very comfortable. Although a smaller car would have done for the two of us, our cost was only about $40.00 a day plus gas.

We arrived at Heathrow at about noon, and by one we were finding our way out of the airport and onto the Motorway (throughway) toward Oxford to the northwest. Of course it takes a bit of time to get used to keeping to the left, and the speeds on the motorways add a bit of extra spice. I got into the slow lane and spent most of the trip there doing between 60 and 70 per. In the middle lane the big truckers passed me steadily, and in the fast lane the smart set on big motorcycles and small, red sports cars whizzed by.

After spending tourist time in Oxford, we went on a few miles to Woodstock. There in this ancient market town we found a small pub-hotel where we got a good room. Local charm is the name of the place, Vickers Hotel. Our room was reasonable in price, but a few doors away was The Bear, a similar but larger pub, which advertises that it has been putting up travelers, rich and poor, for 700 years. We checked their rate and found that they did have a room (no breakfast) at 100 pounds. The English pound then was worth about $1.60, so we left, wondering about the "poor" people who stayed there.

We walked a block or so to the end of the main street and found ourselves at the entrance to Blenheim Palace, the birthplace of Winston Churchill. The grounds here are beautiful with sweeping vistas and a duck-laden lake in front of the old building. We enjoyed walking around the place, and then went back to the Vickers for a dinner of "bar food."

For those of us who don't travel much, English pubs need some special comment. They are by no means just bars, and they are, consistently, the traveler's best friend. All the ones that we tested out in our tour were warm and friendly places fully suitable for family dining in every way. They all serve soft drinks and tea and coffee just as much as beer and ales and wines and other alcoholic beverages. All have tables, and it is rare to find a TV set going or a radio blaring.

Dinners can be very expensive and time-consuming. Much as we love candlelight and atmosphere, on this trip we thought more about the bottom line. So we got used to another aspect of good English pubs, and that is what they call "bar food," or sometimes "bar fare." Bar food usually includes sandwiches and the like, but you also find quite hearty meals on the menu. You place your order for the dish you want. Either the bartender will call out your number when the food is ready, or a bar person will bring the meal to you. The whole arrangement is simple and informal, and you can usually get a good meal for under ten dollars apiece.

The atmosphere in the pubs is almost always quiet and clubby. People are chatting and enjoying peace and relief from the world's bustle. Many pubs have special qualities, such as the Trout Inn at the town of Lechlade, which is on the banks of the Thames at the location of the first set of locks in the river. Upstream from here the Thames quickly becomes a very small stream. From here on down it is a busy waterway with many, many sets of locks.

Although we were committed to a policy of no deadlines and no big cities, life is always better if a few exceptions are made. Who wants to be enslaved to hard-line directives, even if they are your own?

Our first exception was to arrange to arrive at the house of old friends Jim and Nan Eells at 2 p.m. on our second day of touring. We chose Woodstock for our first night because it is a short pull from there to Wellsbourne, where we were to stay with our friends for two nights.

Wellsbourne is near Stratford-upon-Avon, and after a sumptuous banquet chez Eells, we went to a fantastic production of "As You Like It" done as only the Royal Shakespeare Company can do it. Our friends' house is just outside Warwick, with its not-to-be-missed castle, and in our second day of sightseeing, we got to see Tewkesbury Abbey and the Worcester Cathedral.

Our leisurely touring program called for short drives each day, and 50 or 60 miles was the most we accomplished until the very end. In most towns where we stayed, there was a Tourist Information

Office, and these people will not only find you a Bed and Breakfast, they will also book it for you. We had no bad luck using this service, and it meant that we didn't need to worry about rooms for the night.

The "breakfast" that comes with these rooms is an "English breakfast." This usually means eggs, juice, bacon, sausage, toast and coffee or tea. Since we are used to two meals a day, the large breakfasts meant no need for a large lunch, if any at all. The quality of the food served at a B & B is consistently high, and all the hostesses were proud of the job they do.

Some of the B & B's are quite elegant, and others more simple. We found that in the 10 pounds per person range there was always something to be had and the quality was good. If you wish, in many of the B & B's you can pay a bit more and get a room with a private shower, and sometimes with private bath. These last the British call "en suite" accommodations. In the interest of economy, we learned quickly to not worry too much about these details.

Another highlight on our tour was the resort city of Bath. Bath was built up a number of times throughout history. When the Romans invaded, they found that it already had a goddess of the mineral waters. Nevertheless, they built a temple to their own Minerva and a handsome bathing building, which is now quite fully excavated.

In a modern sense the city was built up in the 18th century, and it became fashionable and has been so ever since. We enjoyed a fine B & B right in the center of the city. We were near some of the major sights, and we could easily walk to the baths and to

Bath Abbey, one of the most beautiful churches in England.

In the old part of the city, near the baths and the Abbey and other points of interest, we found the Saracen's Head, an ancient pub in which Charles Dickens lived for a few weeks in 1835. While there, he wrote parts of the "Pickwick Papers," and nowhere is his memory more revered than in this grand old place. It is one of the finest pubs we encountered.

We toured the south part of England in truly leisurely fashion. We got a comfortable start each morning, and began looking for a B & B each day before mid-afternoon. We went into little seaside towns such as Barton-on-Sea and Christchurch. These are the kinds of villages that one sees in picture books about rural England. They are lovely and relaxed.

We got as far west as Weymouth, where the light is really exceptional. Painters, including especially Constable, have loved Weymouth. There our little B & B cost about $40 U.S. for the night, and the next day we headed off for further explorations.

THE HENGES

Stonehenge! The name itself has always thrilled me, and when I saw how easy it would be to get there from Bath, I decided this was the time to do it. Actually it is an easy drive from Bath, and we left the time-honored resort city without undue haste and got to Stonehenge before lunch.

Stonehenge is one of England's oldest sites, and the construction there is still just about incredible. Actually, it is unique. There is nothing else like it anywhere in the world.

The first Stonehenge was an earthwork on this site some 5,000 years ago. As we see it now, we are looking at a circle of enormous stones put up about four thousand years ago. Scholars now conclude that some of these huge stones came from Wales and some came from Marlborough Downs to the north. The stones brought from Wales must have come on rafts around the coast and then across the mouth of the Severn River near what is now Bristol. Afterwards they were brought overland apparently on log rollers.

I will not dwell on Stonehenge since so much has been written about it. But some things seem worth mentioning. First of all, the monument draws over 700,000 visitors annually. Winchester Cathedral draws 500,000 annually. The impact of this many humans on the area is almost frightening. For a while, graffiti were appearing on the stones, and the earth was suffering from so much foot traffic.

Now, the National Trust, which is responsible for this landmark of British history, has roped off the area of the huge stones and created a path around the circle from which visitors can see and photograph. It seems sad and very disappointing, but it is really very wise.

To get to Stonehenge, you drive through beautiful rolling countryside where the large fields are either under cultivation or are given over to grazing. Herds of cattle and flocks of sheep are all around, and then all of a sudden you have arrived. There is a large carpark for cars and tour buses, and an entry area where you buy your entry ticket, find the toilets, and can buy souvenirs. After using those facilities as you wish and need, you go through a tunnel under the road and emerge in the area of the henge itself.

Questions arise in your mind as you walk around this amazing collection of stones. And these questions do not have clear and easy answers. One is, why this spot? Obviously, the site was important to prehistoric man for thousands of years, but why here? There is no water here. This is not an especially high place or an easily defensible one. Why here?

Other questions can be and have been answered by the scholars who have studied Stonehenge. For one thing, it was clearly not a Druid temple. It was probably already in ruins by the time of the Druids in Britain. Other matters, such as the astronomical implications of the placement of the stones, have been studied and written about at great length. The alignment of the double ring of stones is such as to prove full awareness on the part of the builders of the seasonal variations in the rising and setting of the sun in southern Britain.

To stand on this mound and look through and at the stones, and to look off at the horizon, punctuated here and there by barrows, or large mounds that are man-made and no doubt contain the relics of clan leaders, is deeply moving. We were there on a clear and windy day. The countryside is lonely. There are no houses in sight. The land is fertile, but you are alone out there on a rise with the wind, and with these amazing ruins.

Good photographs and a fascinating discussion of Stonehenge are available in most libraries in the book *The Enigma of Stonehenge* by John Fowles and Barry Brukoff.

By the way, you can get to Stonehenge and back in one day from London on a modern, comfortable tour bus. Don't miss it!

Inspired by this great experience, we decided to go on to Avebury, an even larger and in many ways more impressive henge. Avebury lies to the north of Stonehenge, and by road it was only about 25 miles. It seemed longer because the roads are two-laners so you do not want to drive fast, and the countryside is so fascinating that you go slowly just to enjoy it. I have never seen richer farmland, and the fields are large by any standard.

As you approach Avebury you are reminded of the fact that the British have not caught the American fever for promotion. Avebury is discreetly marked with a little road sign, and that's it. No notice about ruins of a great and historic place of worship, or henge. Nothing!

We entered High Street in Avebury going past the Red Lion, a 17th century thatch-roofed inn where later in the day we would have dinner. There is only one other street in Avebury, so the navigation around town was easy.

From the Tourist Information Center we got advice on where to stay. There are only three Bed and Breakfasts in the tiny village of Avebury, and we chose the Old Vicarage, a choice we were very happy with. At this small inn we had a fine room and delightful breakfast for a very reasonable fee. And we could park safely in the front yard.

We were deeply moved by the charm and warmth of our hostess and by the handsome home that has become the Old Vicarage, a wonderful place to know about in Avebury. A few days later I wrote this little set of lines and sent them to the landlady, Mrs. Richard Fry, with our thanks for her gracious hospitality:

> Lucky the weary trav'ler
>> Who finds this Breakfast and Bed.
> Here there is food that pleases
>> And comfortable rest for his head.
>
> Gracious the lovely hostess
>> And handsome all that surrounds.
> Bless'd is the weary trav'ler
>> Who here finds an end to his rounds.

For Mrs. Fry

In 1663 one John Aubrey wrote to Charles II that the splendor of Avebury compares to that of Stonehenge, as does a great cathedral compare to a parish church. We walked for an hour or so through the remains of this huge religious center.

The area of the Avebury henge is awesome. Unlike Stonehenge, you are free here to walk among the stones, climb on them if you wish. Nine hundred acres are encompassed in this protected area, but farming still goes on, and you open animal-proof gates, and close them behind you, as you wander around. Sheep and cattle barely notice you as you enter and leave their grazings.

The henge was constructed four thousand years ago and originally utilized more than 180 large stones weighing up to 60 tons each. The circle of stones was, and is, surrounded by an enormous ditch and beyond it a high mound. The arrangement suggests a fortification, but there is no other evidence for that idea, and the most probable explanation for the construction is that it was a place of worship.

There is a local rumor that one of the stones at Avebury turns round completely at midnight. I asked the barmaid at the Red Lion if she thought that that was true.

"Oh, yes, sir!" she replied, emphatically.

Knowing that another part of the legend is that the movement can only be seen by witches, I asked, "And have you ever seen the stone move?"

"Oh, no, sir!" she replied, even more emphatically. "I've never seen it, meself. But there's lots that has, you may be sure."

I had to choose between staying up 'til midnight to check out the movement myself and getting a good night's sleep. In that lovely rural setting, drowsiness easily overcame ambition, and the need to sleep won out.

The next morning I got up before dawn and wandered through the henge, watching the sun make new and ever-changing patterns as it slowly rose over ancient Avebury. The great power of the impression made by this place probably explains why so much of it was destroyed later during the relentless growth of the new Jerusalem. Christianity, as it grew, did not take kindly to relics of former worshiping.

Outside Avebury, in West Kennet, there is a barrow, or mound, that has been excavated. We drove to that area, and found a lay-by, or parking area beside the road with a small sign and arrow pointing up to a rise at some distance away. We parked and made the journey up to the top of the hill. There we found a tomb, open at one end, and made of the same kind of stones, or sarsens, that were used at Avebury and Stonehenge. We could enter the tomb.

It was an amazing feeling, here at the top of a high hill in an area of rolling countryside, with farmland all around, to find this great monument bequeathed to us by prehistoric man. The tomb is large enough to walk in without hitting your head. It consists of a long corridor, about 20 feet as excavated, with small side chambers on either side.

Outside the entrance of the tomb are three large stones, not closing the entrance, but simply marking it. You walk around them to enter.

Avebury and the West Kennet barrow are almost totally non-commercialized. There is nothing at the West Kennet site other than the markers and a sign explaining the place. Visiting these places gives you a very private experience that is hard to find in our crowded world today.

For our last night of motoring in England, we decided that we should stay near London so that we could get to Heathrow easily the next day and turn in our car. We had got quite far to the west in our wanderings and were in Weymouth, an interesting seaside resort town. We checked the map and found that the city of Staines seemed to be close to London and to Heathrow.

We knew nothing about Staines except that, judging from the map, it was located on the Thames River. We are river lovers and suspected that a city on the Thames could not be all bad. We got up early and drove to Staines, getting there at lunchtime.

During our lunch of bar food at a pub in Staines, we learned from fellow diners that the river was just a few blocks away. After lunch we drove to it, and lo and behold, right there in the middle of this exceedingly dreary industrial city was a riverside pub and hotel that had been there when Samuel Pepys was doing his wandering. It was called the Swan Hotel.

We stayed at the Swan and had a good supper in their bar. Our room looked out on the Thames, and we watched the busy traffic of cruising motorboats and rowing teams. We walked along the river and talked to fishermen. And in the morning we watched the rowers in shells out for their training sessions.

While there we walked along the old tow path at the edge of the Thames and went as far as Runnymede where King John once agreed to the signing of the Magna Carta. We enjoyed the active life along the river—many fishermen, lots of boating, and an occasional pub or two to be investigated.

By choosing to stay in Staines the night before needing to turn in our car at Heathrow, we had avoided the high cost of a motel room at the airport, and we had added one more touristic discovery to our trip.

To say you had a lovely night in Staines, we learned quickly, was about equivalent to claiming a delightful interlude in Hoboken. No one knows about The Swan, and the industrial city of Staines has a perhaps well deserved reputation for being a kind of industrial wasteland.

But the old Swan is delightful. There is fine old woodwork, a workable bath down the hall, a riverfront terrace, and good food to be had. Our room on the second floor faced the river, and we could step out onto a balcony accessible only from our room.

The Swan is located on a little street which is a *cul de sac* and is only a few houses deep. Opposite is another old inn, but it's not on the river so we didn't consider it. Both The Swan and its competition across the street offer evening entertainment and dancing.

We enjoyed listening to a cocktail hour of American jazz music played by a very competent quintet. It was Dixieland at its best, we thought.

From The Swan to Heathrow was a very short fifteen- or twenty-minute drive. We turned in our car

at the airport, shouldered our backpacks, and walked
to the bus area to catch our ride to London for the
next phase of our trip.

LONDON

While we are not exactly what you could call "old London hands," we had been there before, and we felt that we had something of an acquaintanceship going. And of course a lot of the folks there speak English, or at least try to.

At Heathrow, that ghastly and uncomfortable airport, we found the right bus and got aboard. We were on our way to a great adventure in jolly old London Town.

The bus let us off within about ten or twelve blocks from the Alexander, the small hotel at which we had booked a room from the States. We shouldered the backpacks. I grabbed the trusty Olivetti and camera, and we started hiking. Along the way we became a bit suspicious about our directions, and I asked a very friendly telephone man in an official truck for help. He got out a good little directory of streets, and we soon trudged on. Backpacks are the travelers' best friend, we decided, after all, no wait at the airport, no need for a cab, and hiking through London seemed very easy.

Soon we were at a spot we felt had to be close to Sumner Road, our destination, but we didn't see it. I popped into a Deli and asked the girl at the cash register if she knew where Sumner Road might be? "Never heard of it, Love," was her answer. Others who were in the store were apparently as nonplussed as she was, so I stepped out and told Lynn that we might be hopelessly lost.

At this point a cheery chap, who clearly had heard my question inside, tapped me on the shoulder and said, "Sumner Road's right there, and if you're looking for the Alexander, it's the third door on the right." He was pointing to the street directly across from the Deli. In a trice we were at the desk of the elegant Alexander Hotel and found that our reservations were in good shape and we could relax.

Lynn chose to nap for a bit, and I went out and found that the hotel is near a sales office for the legendary Morgan automobile. Morgans, as you may know, are still built in the sporting traditions of the fabulous '30's. They're small, about like the old M.G.s, but racier looking and far more uncomfortable. Actually, the spring suspension dates from the days of buckboards.

I sniffed my way around a fire red model on the sales floor, and finally a chap from the sales office emerged to take my order. I explained that I was a traveler and really not about to purchase a car. I was merely interested. "How much are they?"

The salesman explained that a new Morgan, such as the one on the floor, would cost about $14,000 (I made the conversion from pounds sterling in my head). However, used Morgans are available, and easier to get.

"For a new one the waiting list is about 7 years," he said, rather proudly, I thought. "However, there are plenty of used ones. They cost a lot more, probably over $20,000."

I wandered on, pondering the vagaries of British pricing, and discovered that we were very near the Victoria and Albert Museum, which we wanted to visit, and soon did.

Early that evening we headed across town in a cab to the Vanderbilt Racquet Club, owned and operated by our friends Charles and Susanna Swallow. At the club we were joined by the Swallows' son, Mark, whose new book, "Teaching Little Fang," based on his experiences during a year in mainland China, was just out.

After splitting a bottle of fine Clicquot, we toured the Club and marveled at the extent of its facilities. There are the eight indoor tennis courts, and also a wide variety of workout rooms, squash courts, and other health care necessities, plus a bar and food service.

Later, over dinner at the trendy Columbia Restaurant, Susanna explained that their Club, unlike many London clubs, is open to women, does not require a seven-year wait while your pedigree is checked out, and does not even demand high social status. On the other hand, those who do join are very serious about their game. These people need a relaxing club in which to play and not be "onstage" in a social sense.

The members all love the Club because when they are at it, they are left alone. For example, when we arrived for lunch the next day, at Susanna's urging, we watched Princess Di play her sets for a while. Shortly, she appeared at lunch with the rest of us. There was no rush to surround her. She was relaxed and could behave like just one more guest in the room. Susanna explained that for the Princess, who lives her very hard working life in an unending series of tight schedules and under the intense scrutiny of the press, hours spent at the Vanderbilt Racquet Club are precious ones indeed.

Speaking of Princess Diana, the writer Andrew Morton says, "The Princess is a social player. Her personal coach is owner of the Vanderbilt Club, Old Etonian Charles Swallow, who has improved her game out of all recognition...Club members, who include Adam Faith, John McEnroe and Dustin Hoffman, hardly raise an eyebrow when the Princess arrives to play on one of the eight enclosed indoor courts. It was the Club's discretion which decided Diana to enroll Prince William, who is 'mad keen,' for weekly lessons..."

Since one of my purposes on our trip was to write about the places we would be visiting and to take pictures to illustrate these articles, I had my camera with me at all times. Actually, I took two cameras. One was a modern, computerized, auto focus 35 mm one with a 28 to 85 mm zoom lens, and the other was an Olympus XA, a tiny 35 mm camera which is easy to carry in a hidden way when that seemed wise or convenient.

In London I found first-class processing facilities, but after my pictures were ready, I had to go back to order enlargements of just the right selections. The time taken to go back and forth across the city from our hotel and back again was too much. I decided, with a lot of disappointment, that I would use nothing but color film, and that I would rely on the one-hour shops to do the work.

It was a good decision because everywhere we went there were one-hour shops, and the standards are surprisingly good. The Kodak Gold 100 and 200 film I used was also excellent in its reliability.

Some folks may wonder why not slides? The answer is that slides take longer, require far more precise work, and slides can be made from negative film easily when and as needed and at a later date.

Nineteen eighty-nine was the 150th anniversary year for the invention of photography, and London, like other major European cities, was having fine photography shows. Especially of interest were the shows at the Victoria and Albert and at the Royal Academy of Art. At the first we saw photographs by Clementina, Viscountess Hawarden, and at the latter a large show of representative work by photographers of distinction through the history of the craft. The Hawarden show later came to New York and was widely praised.

There is so much to see in London that it is always a wonderful place to visit. One must not feel overwhelmed by the abundance, but rather one must nibble away, taking full satisfaction from each bite and looking forward to more to come.

I developed my own personal philosophical resolution on this trip. "We should enjoy what we are doing without a thought to what we might be doing in full recognition of the fact that whatever we are doing we would not be doing if we were not doing it." *C'est ça!*

Thus philosophically equipped to enjoy every moment, we got to a play in the West End, no longer the bargain it once was for Americans, but it still has very high standards. We lucked into seeing Anthony Hopkins in "M Butterfly." It was a show we had missed in New York.

Although "M Butterfly" has been a very successful theater piece, I found that I felt that I had been had. The thing is preposterous, if carefully considered. Its success depends on your *not* considering it carefully. This kind of theatrical sleight-of-hand can be, and was, successfully accomplished by Anthony Hopkins.

In carrying off this show, Hopkins once again proved that he is one of the small number of truly great actors of our era. Now he's shocking people with that dumb little piece of nastiness called "The Silence of the Lambs."

"They're not silent enough," quipped a discerning friend. Here's hoping that A. Hopkins will get a meatier role soon. He deserves the finest.

London on this trip gave us the wonderful experiences of catching up with old and dear friends, seeing great shows in fabulous museums, and generally giving us several days of delightful wandering through the interesting by-ways of a great city.

We returned for lunch one day to the Sherlock Holmes Pub, just off Trafalgar Square. We had been there years ago, and we love this veritable museum of the great detective's memorabilia.

As we left London, we reflected upon the fact that we were leaving as one always should leave a place—still excited about it and hoping to get back soon.

SCOTLAND

Our stay in Edinburgh was made absolutely delightful by our hosts, Tom and Joan Dennis and their lovely daughter, Harriet. Tom and I had spent time together in 1949 in Spain as students at the Universidad de Valladolid. Over the years we had kept in touch, and Lynn and I looked forward to seeing him and meeting his family.

They met us at the very airport and whisked us off to their wonderful house where we were treated like visiting royalty for a week.

Edinburgh is a beautiful city and with the Dennises we got to see some of the most delightful parts of it. We went to the theatre one evening and saw "Whisky Galore," which was very well done. Harriet is a devoted theatre person and is deeply involved in Edinburgh's rich theatrical activities. That evening Tom attended a Cricket Association meeting.

One day, while Joan put in her time working at a store that sells things for the benefit of cancer patients, Tom and Lynn and I set off for the town of Linlithgow, which is about 20 miles west of Edinburgh and easy to reach by good roads. Linlithgow Palace, located here, is a magnificent royal edifice and was the birthplace of Mary Queen of Scots. All the Stewart kings lived here, and later it housed Cromwell and Bonnie Prince Charlie.

The palace is huge and located on a hill overlooking a lake. There are enormous rooms, a banquet hall, a chapel and fireplaces large enough to house a Mack truck. It is built like a fortress, and in the center courtyard there is a large, highly ornamental fountain.

Legend has it that in the old days, when the Stewart kings were in residence, the partying was indeed legendary, and the fountain flowed for days with the purest of imported champagne!

I had always wanted to go to Linlithgow because the house I grew up in was named Linlithgow by my father who loved history. He knew that the first man by the name of Hunter in our family to come to this country, was Adam Hunter, who came from Linlithgow. Adam lived in Topsham, Maine, still a town filled with his descendants, and his son, James, born July 13, 1743, was the first white man to be born in Topsham.

A quick glance at the phone book in Linlithgow convinced me that there were so many Hunters there that it would be hopeless to try to find a close cousin of any sort. Later, we looked in the Greater Edinburgh directory and found that there are some eight or nine hundred Hunters listed!

It may not be a clan, but it's obviously a faction, or could be. If we ever unite, my agenda will be to see to it that a roof is put back on the marvelous ruins of Linlithgow Palace. It's a disgrace to the family not to preserve the place more carefully.

Linlithgow Palace is one of the loveliest of historic sites that we saw in all our trip. Sir David Lindsay of the Mount, in his poem "Papyngo" has the king's dying parrot say in appreciation of the palace:

> Adieu Linlithgow, whose palace of plesance
> micht he ane pattern in Portugal and France

As if that were not enough tribute to the glories of this great home, Sir Walter Scott, in his poem "Marmion" gives us Queen Margaret, sitting in her favorite retreat, the chamber of the northwest tower. She is waiting for the King's return:

> His own Queen Margaret, who, in Linlithgow's tower,
> All lonely sat, and wept the weary hour.

She stayed there in the tower until the King, James IV, returned from his ill-advised invasion of England and his thorough and disastrous defeat and death at the battle of Flodden.

Tom knew that the West Port Inn, a superb pub in the heart of town, would serve us a fine lunch, and it did.

After lunch we made our way to Cairnpapple Henge, high on a barren hilltop not far away. We climbed the hill and marveled once again about the motivation of those industrious builders who five or six thousand years ago chose this very spot to do their burrowing and stone building.

Like so many places in England and Scotland, Cairnpapple is not promoted at all. There's a small road sign and that's it. No neon. No hot dog stand. No souvenir shop. Just the high wind blustering us around on the hilltop and a quiet sense of the awesome perdurability of history.

One evening we suggested that we might take the train to Glasgow the next day. We hadn't realized what an affront such a suggestion would be to our hosts. "Nothing to see in Glasgow," and "You haven't yet seen Edinburgh." Right, of course!

Instead, the next day Joan drove us to the center of Edinburgh, and we took a sightseeing tour bus.

Seasoned world travelers may know other ways, but we have always found that a basic tour of the city on a sightseeing bus is a pretty good deal. So we did that, and got to see many of the outstanding features of the city. On our tour you could get off wherever you wanted and get back on again without extra charge. The buses ran every 15 minutes, so we were able to explore without hurrying.

In Edinburgh you must walk down Princes Street. On one side you have a rich array of stores that offer just about everything, and on the other you look across what is almost a ravine and then up to a skyline dominated by Edinburgh Castle.

One of the stores in the lineup was a souvenir shop, and we couldn't resist. I was delighted to find a Hunter plaid tie, and a number of fine pewter gadgets such as key chain ornaments and pins, which bore the Hunter motto, *CURSUM PERFICIO*, a motto not to be overlooked.

We got off the tour bus to explore Edinburgh Castle and were charmed by this ancient fortress. There is a museum of Scots history in the Castle, and the views all around are very good. You have a fine view of the Firth of Forth, and on the other side of it, the legendary Kingdom of Fife.

While at this stop, we went to the Outlook Tower, just outside the Castle, and saw their Camera Obscura, which was first installed in 1853. The tower itself affords more fine views of the city and its surroundings, but the Camera Obscura offers a special treatment of the view. Through its lens a view of the city is received and projected onto a dish around which viewers stand in a darkened room. No camera buff should miss this wonderful apparatus.

For lunch we made our way to Deacon Brodie's Pub in the center of the city. It's a fine pub and a good place for simple fare. Deacon Brodie, the gent for whom the pub was named, was a real Scot of Edinburgh who became the model for Robert Louis Stevenson's "Dr. Jeykell and Mr. Hyde." Ironically, Brodie was the designer of a special trap door device for hangings which was subsequently used in his own hanging, after his conviction for heinous nighttime crimes.

Apartments near the hanging gibbet went for premium prices during the time when the device was used. Who would want to miss a good hanging? The hanging place is visible from the pub.

Later in the day we located Milne's Bar on Hanover Street, just off Princes. This is a legendary hangout of Scots poets, and the walls are filled with pictures of the poets and selections of their poems and a signature or two here and there. Milne's turf is hallowed ground of a sort.

Edinburgh is a city of monuments, and most are worth at least a quick look. The monument to Sir Walter Scott stands elegantly along Princes Street. Its complex gothic design has earned it the title "The Gothic Rocket," but a trip to the top gives you another fine   view of the city.   Also honored by monuments are Admiral Nelson and James Y. Simpson, a pioneer in the use of anesthesia.   Joseph Lister's house is clearly marked and pointed out to you on the tour, as is the home of Robert Louis Stevenson.

Excursions to the environs of Edinburgh are especially wonderful because there is so much that is not   very far away.   For example, about an hour's drive out of Edinburgh you come to Dirleton, a small and very picturesque town with a fine beach nearby, a good hotel pub, a lovely parish church, charming cottages around the village square, and above all, the magnificent Dirleton Castle.

In Dirleton we lunched at the Castle House Hotel, and then toured the castle.   Its architecture is Norman.   It was first built in the 12th century.   It was rebuilt in the 14th century and extended in the 16th century.   At this time, gardens were added to the grounds, which are still remarkable examples of the skill of Scots gardeners.

Dirleton Castle has a deep moat in front of its main entrance.   These days you walk over this on a wooden bridge and then you enter a Norman building that exemplifies all that you have ever dreamed about in Norman design.   Its huge stonework gives no suggestion of frailty, and yet there is no chance overlooked to make the design more handsome or more lovely.   Little touches abound which attest to the great skill in design of these remarkable people.

We walked along the beach at Dirleton, and enjoyed the cool October air.   We went into the parish church, or kirk, which dates from 1612, and was filled with flowers from an earlier wedding.

From Dirleton it's a short drive to Tantallon Castle, which lies about three miles east of North Berwick, if you have a map. If you don't have one, don't worry, you're still very close to Edinburgh.

Tantallon Castle, the ancient and formidable redoubt of the Black Douglas family, is set on the edge of a cliff, and its great curtain wall shuts off the end of the land and creates a safe compound. From the water it was virtually unassailable. From the land you would have to get over this enormous wall, and I decided that no friend of mine would ever try that if I could help it.

Once you get through the wall, you go through a deep gateway which formerly contained a portcullis, and you can walk to the edge of the cliff and enjoy the view. In the not-far distance lies the Bass Rock, a cliff-sided island with a light house on it, which is home to 80,000 nesting couples of Gannets. The air around the Bass Rock is darkened with their flights. Tantallon Castle was a stronghold, and its massive 50-foot high 14th century curtain wall made it an impregnable place of retreat in times of trouble.

Tom and Joan presided over our visit to Scotland as Prospero did his magical island. We would never have had the sense of the place as well without them.

I think the average traveler entering a new country with just a few days to spend there would be wise to stay put. But we were lucky enough to get around a lot.

"You cannot leave without seeing the Highlands, even if only a bit." By this time, we knew that when

Joan said that, she meant that she and Tom were going to get us there. And they did.

Our Highlands excursion was an easy one-day drive from Edinburgh. We left in mid-morning and took the bridge over the Firth of Forth. We went through Dumfermline, birthplace of Andrew Carnegie, and on to Dunkeld. Near Dunkeld is Birnam Wood, made famous in the play "Macbeth." We lunched at the Royal Dunkeld Hotel. The town is simple but nice and tidy. We went into the Athol Gallery, a fine art gallery, and strolled through the town enjoying the clear air of the Highlands.

Even this short excursion gave us newcomers to Scotland an idea of the majesty and rugged fascination of the Highlands. We drove through country like nothing we had ever seen, spooking pheasant and grouse all along, and wishing we had time to fish the little trout-laden streams we saw.

Back to myth smashing. Haggis has always been described to me as the symbol of a masochistic side of the Scottish temperament. "Don't even dream of trying it!" a friend had told us, with a shudder. "Yuck!" sneered another.

But Joan and Tom made sure that we tried it, and we loved it. Maybe it's bad in pubs and at steam tables, but as served *chez* Dennis in Edinburgh, it's a memorable taste treat.

Our final supper with the Dennises was memorable not only because of the fine haggis, but mostly and mainly because it was a chance to say goodbye to our new-old friends in a quiet and leisurely way.

Dirleton Castle is one of the finest of the Norman Castles in Scotland. It seemed absolutely lovely to us.

The Cocteau Chapel sits right at the water's edge in Villefranche sur Mer, and near the Hotel Welcome.

AMSTERDAM

The flights that took us from Edinburgh to Amsterdam, via Heathrow in London, were easy and uneventful (always good news). A major factor in our deciding to stop in Amsterdam on this trip was our plan to see our friend, the distinguished Dutch photographer, Rushka Teekema.

Rushka lived in the States for many years when her husband, Rolf, was in business here. During that time she joined the Silvermine Guild of Artists in New Canaan, Connecticut, and it was through the Guild that I first met her.

Lo and behold, when we got to our little hotel, The Estherea, there was Rushka to greet us and be sure we were comfortably established.

In the next couple of days we visited museums with Rushka and saw wonderful shows of photography, all of which were going on as a part of the international celebration of the 150-year birthday of photography.

One afternoon we got to the exhibit at the Canon Image Center. We went up to the little gallery maintained there and saw a dozen or so large, black and white and very explicit shots of women, in various states of disarray and deshabille, using needles to inject drugs.

Generally Amsterdam is a cheery and charming city, but this grim reminder of the undercurrents was not the only one.

At the Reiksmuseum we paid a call on Mrs. Ivoline Uitenhage de Mist, the Curator of Old Coins, and sister-in-law of our Stateside friend June Verspyck.

This delightful and elegant lady greeted us warmly. In the course of our chat with her, she asked us if we had been bothered by approaches from drug dealers. We had not, and in answer to my query she admitted that she had not either. But the matter is on everyone's mind.

Amsterdam deserves an extended period of time. We could not give it that, so we grabbed what we could on the run. We saw the Anne Frank house, and we toured the city through the canals in a water bus. In the evening we went to a deservedly renowned restaurant called Restaurant D'Vijff Vlieghen (The Five Flies). There we had a first-class meal in handsome surroundings. Reservations needed!

The restaurant is located very near our hotel, as was a bookstore whose name intrigued, *Au Bout de Monde*! I was reminded of, but did not seek out, Camus' Bar Mexico City.

One afternoon Rolf and Rushka picked us up in his Ford Granada, and we drove out into the country to the little fishing village of Volendam. The fleet was coming in as we got there, and Rushka and I snapped away, recording images of the picturesque scene.

As we ate fresh herring from a street vendor's cart, we saw a man in traditional, old-fashioned Dutch garb. Rolf explained that this man is usually around, and his photograph in costume appears on a postcard sold everywhere.

In Marken, an island now joined to the mainland by a dike, we had tea at a seaside restaurant, very spanking clean and friendly, and then headed back to the city for a sumptuous feast at the Teekema apartment. "Teekema is a Frisian name," said Rolf, referring to the islands just off the coast of The Netherlands, whose unique language is something like a cross between English and Dutch.

The Teekema family had been planters in Indonesia, and the apartment is filled with fine furnishings from that exotic area. We luxuriated in the warmth of the hospitality of these wonderful friends, and headed off the next day by train to Paris.

PARIS

Think of it this way. When God wanted to create something of the greatest possible beauty, He created France, and when the French people wanted to create something of the greatest possible beauty, they created Paris.

And of course they are still creating it. Les Halles, for example, was always a fascinating market in the old days, and is now a fascinating park. The French have an unequalled genius for steadily improving the great old city. They save what is really fine, and clear out what needs to be eliminated.

We should follow their example. Compare the disappointing way in which St. John's Cathedral in New York faces out onto truck-ridden Amsterdam Avenue and then onto mean streets, to the way Notre Dame is enhanced by the fine park in front of it from which you get a great view of the façade.

It wasn't always that way. The French have made this clearing a fact. One senses, in Paris, that there is a communal, historically unending, mastermind of intelligence that cares for and nurtures the artifact that Paris is. It was, is and always will be, the flower of the finest parts of our collective traditions and accomplishments in the western world.

The visit was made sensationally comfortable by the fact that my student and our good friend, Ellie Robert, on hearing of our plan to visit the city, said, "Here are the keys. Please stay in our apartment!"

Thus it was that we stayed on the Rue Chanoinesse on the Isle de la Cité, and in the very shadow of Nôtre Dame. The Robert apartment is small and cheery and convenient to all sorts of things that we wanted to do and see. The Roberts maintain the apartment for business, but from time to time it sits empty and they love to have friends use it.

The day we left, new arrivals from Montreal put their bags in the front hall even as we were doing a final cleaning of the living room. Generosity is surely the most lovable trait people have, and we wallowed in its benefits.

A favorite book years ago was "The Narrow Street," by Elliott Paul, the Paris Tribune writer. In it he depicts life on the little Rue de la Huchette, just across the Seine on the *Rive Gauche*. It is a charming book.

In the early 1970s we were in Paris and went to the Rue de la Huchette to see what was going on there in present times. We saw hippies galore, and many ladies of the evening parading their bodies in scant attire. One, a young American girl, approached us and suggested a *jou à trois!*

The street Elliott Paul described was quite different. It was respectable and bourgeois, even though the hotel at the corner was indeed a *bordello.*

This time we went to the Rue de la Huchette to see if things had changed. The old hotel in the center of the block was still advertising its cellars, which descend, one beneath the other, into the very bowels of Paris. But the big news was that the Greeks have moved in, and the entire street is one

Greek restaurant after another. The place is a relocated *placa*, ripped away from Athens itself!

The following year our daughter Julie stayed in Paris in the guest room of friends in an apartment in the 16th Arrondissement. Monsieur Louis Dalin and his wife are old friends of Julie's grandmother, Rhoda Truax.

Now you should know that M. Dalin was captured by the Germans in World War II, and later escaped from his prisoner of war camp. Also interesting is the fact that Louis Dalin's father was captured by the Bosch in W.W.I, and (hold on!) the *grandfather* of Louis Dalin was captured by the Huns in the Franco-Prussian War!

This astonishing record combined with the distinguished career of M. Dalin has led to his becoming president of the Escaped Prisoners of France, a proud and active group of French veterans.

Subsequently Julie moved on to take up digs in another apartment, and one day Julie received a call from M. Dalin. "Could you join me on Sunday next for an outing?" was the esteemed gentleman's query. *"Mais certainement!"* was fair Julie's reply, and that's how it all started.

Now on this specific Sunday under scrutiny here, M. Dalin marched at the head of a parade that took over the Champs Elysées. All traffic was routed away from that grand boulevard, and the parade was watched by thousands of cheering Parisians.

At the head of the parade marched M. Dalin, and on his right arm was Juliana!

At the Place de l'Etoile, Generals were as common as fleas on a hog's back, and all were introduced to Julie and expressed their enchantment

at the opportunity to meet *cette belle Americaine.*
The occasion was of highest importance in the
Histoire de la Gloire de la Republique Française, of
course. President Mitterand, also an escaped prisoner,
was supposed to have been there, but could not
make it.

Newspaper photographers were as common
as general officers at this gathering, and limousines
were everywhere. Flags flew, cameras clicked, and
the Marseillaise brought tears to the eyes of the
multitudes.

And in this scene of great patriotic fervor
and highly emotional arousement, who else but
Julie stepped forward and laid the wreath on the
Tomb of the Unknown Soldier? No one else! She
did!

And as we say, *Allons enfants,* what else is
new?

For all three of us a special treat was lunch
one day, with suburban Parisians who are old
friends of Jeff and Kate Hedges, our near kin here in
the East. These suburbans are Claude and Fanny
Gâteaux who live in Villennes sur Seine, twenty
minutes away from town on the train from Gare St.
Lazarre.

Claude and Fanny and their four children live
in a fine Victorian chateau, which is utterly charming.
We were treated to a wonderful Provençal-style
midday meal, which meant course after course of
delicious food and fine Provençal wine.

Throughout our trip we kept learning new
dimensions of hospitality, and nowhere more than
in France. The old French saying, *Ma maison est
votre maison* (subsequently appropriated by the
Spanish, of course) was never truer.

"We are away from our house from July 15 to the end of August. Please come and stay in it. We want you to," said Claude on a recent visit to the States. He was repeating the offer made earlier. Some day, maybe...

While in France I wrote an article for publication in the States, and I will reprint the text here. It was as follows:

Everyone loves Paris in the springtime. It's a well-known fact, and it's a song. But do not limit your thinking to just that season. Paris is a delight at any time of year, and an absolutely astonishing number of exciting and worthwhile offerings are always there to select from. Paris is truly a "City for all Seasons."

We in North America owe so much to the culture of France that a visit to its capital is always a refreshing reminder of the greatness of the people and their culture.

Paris is delightful in any season and in almost any weather. Perhaps no other city in the world lets you have the outside while still being inside. Impossible? No, not with the outdoor cafes that abound in Paris. Your table seems to be out, but it's really in and heated, if needed.

Over 400 art galleries beckon, restaurants offer the finest of a wide variety of foods, and the more than 50 museums present a sensational array of new and old art and artifacts to satisfy the art lover's yearnings for months (if there were time).

Of course, there are many famous sights that you will not want to miss. A good guide book, such as the famous Michelin Tourist Guide in English will be needed to remind yourself of the major sights and to help you make a reasonable list of things to see while you are there. You will find yourself choosing from places like the Louvre Museum, the new and exciting Museum d'Orsay, Napoleon's Tomb, the Picasso Museum and dozens upon dozens of others.

If you have never been to Paris before, you will find it valuable to take a half-day bus tour around the city. These tours are cheap and well run, and an English-speaking guide will point out interesting sights to you all the way.

With this embarrassment of riches, and with a desire to keep expenses under control, the problem becomes, "How to do a visit to Paris without getting exhausted and without going broke?"

Start by finding a hotel that is reasonable and that is convenient to where you would like to be most of the time. If you are unfamiliar with Paris, get advice from a travel agent. A book which will give you the names of reasonable hotels, many costing well under fifty dollars per night per person, is called "Hotels de Charme de Paris," published by Rivages in 1990. Good small hotels abound, and Paris is generally a safe city.

As to getting around in the city, keep the Métro (subway) in mind. It is easy to use, even for non-French speakers, and it is cheap. If you buy packs of ten tickets, called "carnets," each ride costs about $.65. The Métro is fast, clean and safe. Many cars travel on rubber tires and thus the usual roar of subways is pleasantly muted.

So, ensconced in a clean, tidy and charming hotel, you set forth by Métro to see exciting sights and have wonderful meals. The Métro trains are listed by their Direction, or destination. Pocket maps are free, and large maps are displayed outside and inside every station.

Take the train marked Pont de Neuilly. This train will take you in short order to the western edge of Paris, near the huge park called the Bois de Bologne.

At the end of its run you come up on the Avenue Charles de Gaulle, and from here you can walk to the Bois de Bologne or walk farther west on Charles de Gaulle. Walking this way will take you to La Defense, a brand-new commercial low-rise skyscraper office building complex.

Surrounding the great La Defense itself, world-famous architects have realized a cluster of buildings that present a breathtaking array of the finest of modern design.

The Grand Arch at La Defense is huge. Its interior opening is large enough to house Nôtre Dame including its spires! The arch has office suites inside it, and its roof area is open to the public. A quick elevator ride takes you to the top from which you can see Paris spread out before you.

Looking back toward the Place de l'Etoile, you see the Eiffel Tower to the right, with an enormous high-rise office building at Montparnasse beyond. In the distance at the left is Sacre Coeur, shining away on its own hilltop, the fabled Montmartre.

In keeping with the grandness of gesture that makes Paris the sensational city that it is, La Defense, which celebrates the defense of the city in 1871 and throughout the course of its history, is the center of a spectacular new part of Paris.

The arch was designed by a Danish architect, John Otto von Spreckelsen. It stands as the newest landmark on the historic axis which runs from the Louvre Museum, up Champs Elyssées Avenue to the Place de l'Etoile, along Charles de Gaulle Avenue and to the center of the new La Defense business district.

As you get out of the Métro on your way to La Defense, you will find yourself near a Pizza Hut. Of course, you did not go to Paris to eat American food, but give it a try. Many of the seats at this hi-tech restaurant look out upon an enclosed garden in the finest Parisian tradition, and the waitresses use a gadget similar to a TV control unit to beam your order to the kitchen. The service is good, and the food is good, too.

Another easy ride on the Métro from your downtown hotel will be the one to the Père Lachaise Cemetery. This large (over 100 acres) wooded cemetery is the resting place of many distinguished heroes of the distant and recent past. Here are the graves of Moliere, Balzac,

Proust, Chopin, Piaf, Bernhardt, Collette and Jim Morrison.

Although the cemetery seems awfully run down in some areas, the overall effect is fascinating. Crypts and mausoleums butt up against each other in a crowded way, but the paths are lovely and tree-lined. The cemetery is a fine place to get in touch with the Paris of the past and sense the receptiveness of this great city to the talents of those who have been important here.

Jim Morrison, known for his singing leadership of the rock group The Doors, is buried in a rather hidden-away spot which would be easy to miss except for the signs scratched in the walls here and there which display an arrow and the word, "Jim." Once there, you are apt to find followers gathered paying tribute in sometimes rather hippy fashion.

It is impressive that Morrison, who died 20 years ago, still attracts a steady procession of devoted lovers of his work. As a young friend said recently, "A visit to Morrison's grave is a ritual sacred to our era." Sacred, or very much not so, the trip is worth the time.

On your way to Morrison's grave, you may be stopped by someone who is mapless (maps are available at the cemetery entrance). A young man who saw me studying my map came up and queried, "Have you seen Chopin?"

Where else?

Although sewers may not seem like a major

attraction, it is nevertheless true that the sewer system of Paris is a marvel not to be missed. You enter through a stairway at the Place de la Résistance, and you are entering a veritable "city beneath a city."

Every major street in Paris has at least one and sometimes two sewer tunnels under it. Intersections in the tunnels are marked just as are the street intersections above. Signs clearly tell you just where you are.

The system was built, in the main, in the 19th century, and the great excitement it aroused inspired Victor Hugo to include many scenes in his novel, "Les Miserables," in which the hero, Jean Valjean, makes his way safely around the city using the sewers as his hiding place.

What the tourist sees in the sewer system is enough to explain how the whole system works, and there is a fine set of explanatory materials in the form of large charts with historical information on them. The trip is not unpleasant in the way you might fear. It is fascinating to learn about, and the cost of the visit is minimal.

The cost of eating in Paris can be outrageous, or it can be kept under control. Many of even the least expensive hotels offer coffee and bread of some kind for breakfast. Lunches can be made of sandwiches which are sold everywhere. Or a simple lunch at small and simple restaurants can be reasonable in price.

Dinners provide a greater challenge. The temptation is to go to exciting special places like the Taverne du Sergeant Recruteur on the Ile St. Louis, or Le Pied de Cochon just off the park which used to be the market area called Les Halles. Either of these, and many, many more, are exciting, fun, and not too bad in price as compared to a good American restaurant. Dinner will cost 30 to 40 dollars apiece, but if you have scrimped successfully on the two earlier meals, maybe your attitude will be, "Why not?"

A good area to search out bargain meals in is the old Latin Quarter, on the Left Bank. Pay your necessary visit to Nôtre Dame, and then go to the Left Bank, a short walk across the bridge. There you will find yourself in a warren of cafes and restaurants, many old and distinguished, and many which have sprung up recently.

If you choose to try a fine and probably crowded restaurant, be sure to call ahead for a reservation. You will most likely hear an English-speaking voice at the other end of the line. If not, they will find someone quickly who can make your booking. Probably your table will be ready when you arrive.

Paris is the flower of Western Europe. No other city in the world is as elegant, and on this trip we found the French to be very receptive to visitors. Parisians love to enjoy life, and the city is set up to be enjoyed. Each view is more lovely than the last, each square more imposing or more intriguing than the last. Perhaps none outshines the lovely Place des Vosges, the oldest square in Paris.

Parisians are busy and hard-working people. Somehow they run a city in which the services such as bus and subway are marvelous, the police are incredibly polite and helpful, and the streets are safe for strolling at any time of day.

Most importantly, keep in mind that in visiting Paris you cannot do it all. Do not miss the fact that leisure can be enjoyed in Paris as in no other place in the world. Take your time. Make each excursion an event of its own, and don't try to knock off thirteen major sightseeing events in one day— take six days and linger over your after-dinner coffee.

When it came to leaving Paris, we shouldered our backpacks and walked to the nearby Hotel de Ville subway stop, and two stations later we were at the Gare de Sud. We had booked first-class tickets for once, and looked forward to the ride on the T.G.V., the Tren a Gran Vitesse, of which the French are so proud.

Our seats were super comfortable, the views were lovely, the hostess was the same, and the mid-day dinner was one of the best of our entire trip. Lynn never leaves home without her French wine bottle opener, and we were amused to see that the hostess could not find her opener. Lynn loaned her ours, and the trip went on.

There was only one stop between Paris and Marseilles, and the train achieves really high speeds (over 125 mph) at times. But there is no sensation of discomfort, and we relaxed and enjoyed the posh experience while reliving many of the fabulous pieces of good luck that had made Paris so special for us on this trip.

THE COTE D'AZUR

We love off-season resorts, and we were glad to be going to the South of France to savor some of the fine museums and art treasures without fighting tourist crowds and overbooked hotels and restaurants.

We left Paris on the T.G.V., the fast train from Paris to Marseilles on October 19, 1989. The train reaches speeds of up to 125 miles per hour, but never vibrates or gives any unpleasant suggestion of its great speed. Lunch was served by a uniformed hostess, and it was one of the most memorable meals that this trip to France gave us.

In Marseilles we walked to the front of the train and saw the Avis office near at hand. Within minutes we were in our Renault 19 four-door sedan, which quickly revealed its amazingly fine qualities.

Our first stop on the Côte d'Azur was in Cassis, a tiny fishing and resort port about 20 miles east of Marseilles. This little town has nothing to do with the Cassis liqueur, but it is picture postcard perfect if you are looking for local charm. We were up for that, and we loved it.

We booked into a little hotel and learned that it hadn't rained for months, but then came the downpour! It was very intense, but also very brief, and after it ended, we walked down to the water's edge to see the town. The water was flowing like rivers in the streets coming down the hill, so we had to wade to get across them.

The next day we drove on eastward, through another lovely little resort town, Bandol, and then on to St. Tropez.

Our first museum stop was here. We stayed at the Hotel Bella Vista up the hill from the center of town. It is a comfortable hotel with lovely views over the countryside and out to the water. It is also located on the road to the beaches for which the St. Tropez region is so deservedly famous.

The museum in St. Tropez is the Musée de L'Annonciade, which is located right at the waterfront in a former chapel built at the start of the 16th century. The museum's present collection features art of the twentieth century. Painters included are Matisse, Seurat, Utrillo, Van Dongen, Dufy and a host of others. Two massive Maillol statues dominate the scene on each of the two floors. The collection is colorful and thoroughly delightful.

Before leaving St. Tropez, we spent a half day at Tahiti Beach, one of the long row of beaches south of the town, and we found it in use by a small number of sunbathers and some swimmers. The sun was hot at the time of our late fall visit, and sunbathing was still popular.

In Antibes we stayed at the Hotel Royal which is on the waterfront. Its beach is right in front of it, and we were able to have lunch there while enjoying more of the hot sun of the Côte d'Azur.

The next morning we went up into the hills, away from the shore, to the tiny hill town of St. Paul de Vence. This picturesque little village sits on top of a hill. The oldest parts of the town are within its fortress walls. The streets are narrow and winding and the little shops offer all kinds of items for those who like shopping.

We had post office work to do, and we got that done just outside the old walled town, but still in St. Paul. Then we walked to the Auberge La Colombe d'Or, which is also outside the walls. We were able to make a lunch reservation for one o'clock, and we strolled through the old town until then.

Lunch at the Colombe d'Or was served on the terrace outside the old inn, perched above a valley. The terrace is dominated by a large Leger mural, one of the many art treasures here at this remarkable hotel.

The lunch was superb but not cheap. After we had enjoyed that part of the visit, we went inside and toured the many rooms on the main and second floors, all of which are filled with an amazing array of modern art. Inside there are works by Leger, Matisse, Bonnard, Calder and many, many others. A large Calder mobile dominates one corner of the patio, which also includes the swimming pool.

Inside there are many Calder sketches and small pieces, and two rooms are completely filled with Calder paintings and drawings. Many of these are inscribed to Madame Roux, the owner of the auberge. Although the Colombe d'Or is not officially a museum, it belongs on a tour of museums in southern France.

We went on from there to Vence which is only a few miles away, and there we stayed at Hotel Mas de Vence. Mas is a local Provençal term meaning house, inn or farmhouse. This hotel is a five-star one in my book. It is absolutely first class. Some may find it lacking in charm since it is a lot like a good American motel, but its location on the edge of town, its nearness to the old city, and its first rate qualities in every regard make it a fine place to stay.

In Vence we went to the Matisse Chapel, or more correctly the Chapel of the Rosary, which was planned and carried out by Henri Matisse. It was completed and sanctified by the Bishop of Nice in June of 1951.

Matisse said, "Simple colors can act on the inner feelings all the more powerfully as they are simple." This chapel is a monument to this concept, and it seems vibrant and somehow pure and simple. Tall glass windows face to the south and receive the bright sun of Provence. In the window design, yellow and blue leaves stand out against a background of light blue. The room glows.

The murals that Matisse created for this chapel are also starkly simple. The stations of the cross are depicted on one wall in the simplest of outline forms, almost stick figures.

It is important in visiting these museums to ascertain open times before making detailed plans. We had learned that the Matisse Chapel would be open on Tuesdays, and we therefore arrived in Vence on Monday.

After our visit to the Matisse Chapel, we came down out of the hills and through Nice and right on into nearby Villefranche sur Mer.

The distance from Nice to Monte Carlo is less than 20 miles, and in between lie Cap Ferrat, Beaulieu and Villefranche. The first of these as you go east from Nice is Villefranche, and we chose this for our last stop on our short museum tour of the Côte d'Azur.

We learned about Villefranche sur Mer and the Hotel Welcome from a German traveling salesman whom we met in a motorcycle bar in Antibes, that we happened into one evening. Draped over the bar in this dingy place, this teutonic romantic aroused our curiosity about Villefranche. This man had all the yearnings for the South that northerners all over seem to have, and he *loved* little Villefranche. We did, too, when we saw it, and we felt that here we had found a nest to which we would always love to return. Villefranche sur Mer is a tiny town built on the hills that rise abruptly from the sea in the form of an almost perfect semicircle. We stayed at the Hotel Welcome, which is right on the water. Our balcony overlooked the harbor, and just under us were fishing boats, coming and going, and nets spread out to dry on the pavement.

As you go past the Hotel Welcome, you are on the road (which is a dead end for cars) that takes you along the beach at the head of the harbor and then on to a parking area. From there you look back at the city with its huge waterfront castle built in the 16th century by Philibert, Duke of Savoy. The town is picture perfect, and the beach, which faces south, was a busy place with sunbathers lined up to enjoy the still-hot rays.

On the beach the topless ladies baked their bodies every day. The tourist season was about over, and we noticed that the same people showed up each day, and took about the same position. There was the tall, slim blonde, who would sit down, each afternoon at about 1:30, remove her top, and then lie back to absorb the rays. Another lady was fiftyish and a bit overweight, but marvelously architected. I suspected that in an earlier time she must have been a model. Her total lack of self-consciousness was refreshing.

The "Watermelon Lady" was most amusing. She was in her seventies, wore a little fussy hat, and transparent silk panties. Her breasts were enormous, and still quite lovely, I thought.

One afternoon the perfection of the little beach was smeared by chunks of oil spill that were here and there at the water's edge. As I stepped in, in a gingerly way, the "Watermelon Lady" came over and we discussed the unhappy condition of the beach. At least, I think that was what we were talking about. My French was still rusty at that point. She was quite cheery, quite decorative, and very friendly. Why aren't American grandmothers like that?

Later we decided to have dinner at a quai-side restaurant, and we were given a table for two. Although the restaurant was nearly empty, the waiter, in true French fashion, put us at a table inches away from another two-seater with a single man seated at it.

Generally, I assume that people at the next table are speaking a language I don't understand, so I pay no attention. But Lynn, quick as a wink, realized that this guy was parlaying English with the waiter, and quite well at that.

We fell into conversation with this man, whose name is Bosse Lindahl, and learned that he is from Stockholm and was getting a bit of a break from his busy life there as a restauranteur.

Small World Department: "Stockholm?" said Lynn. "Perhaps you know our friend Bengt Oldmark."

"But of course I know Bengt," said our new friend from Sweden. "I know him very well. I buy large quantities of provender from him."

Bengt is in the wholesale food business in Stockholm. So that is how we made a new friend in Stockholm. Bosse Lindahl's restaurant, Tullgarns Vardshus is high on our list of not-to-be-missed dinner spots. Some day.

Across the street from the Hotel Welcome, and virtually at the water's edge, is the tiny Chapelle St. Pierre, now known at the Cocteau Chapel. Jean Cocteau, the French man of all arts, was a lover of the Hotel Welcome, and some years ago decorated the chapel. It is a fascinating work of art now, and definitely is worth the time it takes to get there to enjoy it.

In the summertime the South of France churns with tourism. You line up to get into museums, and you must reserve space at restaurants way ahead. But in the fall, you call your own shots. We found the uncrowded and unhurried pace of our museum tour to be just the relaxing vacation time that most of us want but cannot always achieve.

TURKEY

Any report on our experiences in Turkey has to start back in New York, when I was a graduate student at N.Y.U. One day back then I wandered into the student center and had the good fortune to sit at a table with a young Turkish chap named Tufan Cankat.

Tufan and I fell into conversation, and I invited him to my fortieth birthday party, which was coming up in a couple of days. He came, we got to know him as the months went by, and we kept up by mail after he went home.

Years later, in 1985, Lynn and I, and Dan and Kathy and Julie visited Tufan in Istanbul. Talk about rolling out the carpet! Tufan's welcome was incredible. For almost a week he hosted us and guided us through the city, moving about with great ease in his car with its attentive driver. We luxuriated. Since he wouldn't hear of our staying in a hotel, he gave us his apartment, complete with its friendly maid who served us meals and took care of our laundry!

On this trip we stayed once again in his extremely comfortable apartment on the European side of Istanbul. Shortly after arriving, we set out on a wonderful tour in Tufan's car. There were five of us on the trip—Tufan, his wife Fusun, Lynn and me and the driver. The article which follows first appeared in the weekend edition of the *Turkish Daily News*, a large English-language newspaper published in Istanbul.

Tufan placed the article for me, and I was pleased to know that he liked it. There are hardly enough ways to express our gratitude for all that Tufan has done for us in Turkey on these trips.

The article reports on many of the experiences we had, but fails, of course, to include mention of the warmth of the reception we received. In Yalova, for example, we stopped and went up to Tufan's beachside condo, a delightful retreat.

After our trip up the mountain Uludag, in the funicular, and our fabulous dinner on high, we returned to Yalova and stayed overnight at the apartment of Tufan's nephew, the jeweler. He, Cengiz Kalacyoglu, and his wife Senay and their lovable children made us feel completely at home. The kids proudly spoke some of their excellent English, and Senay treated us to a fine meal.

Breakfast at the Kalacyoglu apartment, which overlooks the Sea of Marmara, was fabulous. It consisted of soft-boiled eggs, cheese, bread, lamb hot dogs, salami, and two kinds of olives! No one left the table hungry.

Tufan and Fusun, in their generous way, had included us in the trip even though the major purpose was to attend the engagement party of the son of a friend of Fusun.

We arrived at the Buyuk Truva, our hotel in Cannakale on the Dardanelles, in time for a nap and a shower, and then we attended what turned out to be an enormous dinner party with lots of dancing interspersed. Hundreds of people were seated in the grand ballroom of the hotel, and we had never seen so many flowers in our lives!

The flower arrangements were enormous. They were seven or eight feel tall, mounted on stands, something like easels, and they were everywhere. Turkey is a land of flowers, and it seemed that they were all there that night.

We enjoyed the party, given in honor of this handsome young couple. We were warmly accepted. Along about 11 in the evening we decided that, after untold numbers of courses, we had to excuse ourselves and get to bed. The next day Tufan told us that the dinner had gone on a lot longer, ending with a soup course at about one o'clock in the morning.

My article includes none of these personal notes, but here's what they ran.

Istanbul is the crown jewel of Turkey and one of the world's most fascinating cities. Sited as it is on the shores of the Bosphorus, Istanbul is partly in Europe and partly in Asia. Nowhere else can you visit a city which, while thoroughly European in many ways, is also placed in Asia Minor and has all the charms of a cultural heritage that is very different from what Westerners are used to.

When you visit Istanbul, do not fail to set aside many days, if possible, to see the amazing and delightful sights that this city offers.

Topkapi, Santa Sophia, the ancient covered markets and the spice market nearby are merely starters in a long list. A good idea is to get a travel guide book and pore over the possibilities. Surely no one should miss the Blue Mosque of Sultan Ahmet (near Santa Sophia) or the Suleymaniye Mosque near the University.

The ancient city walls beckon, and the ferries on the Bosphorus are cheap and beautiful and very enjoyable. Ferry boats can take you up the Bosphorus, across to Asia, or out to the Prince's Islands. All these trips are worth the time, if you can possibly stay in Istanbul long enough.

Turkey is a large country, bigger than Texas, and extremely varied as to terrain and climate. We left Istanbul and traveled by road to Izmit at the eastern end of the Sea of Marmara. After Izmit we headed west along the south shore of that body of water and made our first stop in Yalova.

Yalova is a bustling small city with lovely apartment houses along the water's edge and frequent ferry service to Istanbul. Here we were befriended by a local goldsmith who has a fine jewelry store at which we bought, at an exceptionally good price, a pair of Turkish gold earrings for my wife. The store, called Cengiz, is owned by the talented Cengiz Kalacyoglu, a remarkable craftsman.

There are thermal baths in Yalova dating back to Roman times. The great early 20th century leader of Turkey, and its great modernizer, Ataturk, loved the baths and ordered a cottage built for himself there. Now you can visit it, and you can also stay at a reasonable charge at one of the two hotels near the baths.

We took the bus from Yalova, and our new friend made sure we got on the right bus. Actually, it's a good idea to have your destination written out when you travel by bus. In Turkey, English is taught to almost all school children, and tourist-oriented people all speak some English, but be on the safe side.

The buses are good ones, modern, clean and staffed by a driver and a steward. You buy your ticket in the depot and are assigned a reserved seat. You can book the day before if you wish. Once the bus starts, the steward will come by with aromatic water to use on your hands and face. Very pleasant! And if you need drinking water, you ask for "su" and he brings you a small bottle.

We travelled farther west to Bursa and there took the cable cars to the top of Uludag, the mountain the ancient Greeks called the Mount Olympus of Asia. In November skiing had just started at the very top, but we stopped at the lodge at the top of the second cable car's run.

There we enjoyed a very special feast for eyes and stomach. In this alpine-style center, lamb meat is cut to your order in your view, and fires are started for you to do your own barbecue cooking. Smoke fills the air and busy, shouting waiters bring your meat to you, along with other items you order, such as yogurt, salad, soup, soft drinks and wonderful Turkish bread.

On the way up the mountain in a cable car, we enjoyed the fabulous view of Bursa as we rose steeply above it. After dark, coming down, the city sparkled before us. The trip is a treat!

From Bursa we traveled westward to the fishing town of Bandirma where we had a fine fresh fish lunch right on the waterfront. From there we went on to Cannakale.

Cannakale is a sleepy town located at the Dardanelles, the Hellespont of antiquity. On the opposite shore the World War I Battle of Gallipoli was fought. There is now ferry service to the European side, and visitors come to Cannakale on their way to the ruins of the ancient city of Troy.

We stayed at the fine Hotel Truva, almost on the waterfront. The promenade along the water's edge takes you to a number of good seafood restaurants for leisurely dining in the Turkish style.

We got up early in Cannakale and went by car to the ruins of Troy. It was a thrill to actually tread on this fabled ground. The excavations are interesting, although not as thoroughly done as one might expect. It is clear from the ruins that many different cities were built on this site. Not only are there the old ruins of Ilium, but there are also Greek and Roman remains of importance.

Jarring notes are struck by the signs directing you to Helen's Restaurant and the looming, wooden Trojan horse built near the entrance to the dig. We climbed up into the horse, of course, but it does not afford an exceptional view.

We traveled south to Ismir, the Smyrna of

biblical times, and there treated ourselves to a night in the Grand Efes Hotel, a five-star hotel of very modern design. We were delighted to find a post office in the lobby, and noted that the signs above the counters are in English.

Izmir is a bustling and prosperous city with tree-lined boulevards and glass and steel buildings. Our hotel overlooked Ataturk Square and the waterfront promenade. Here, as to be expected in a coastal city, are a number of first-class seafood restaurants.

The Turks are justifiably proud of their food. They say, "In the world there are three great cuisines—the French, the Chinese and the Turkish." Be advised that they may well be right! You can count on the best at these waterfront cafés in Izmir, and we dined well with fine Turkish wines as an accompaniment.

We noted at these restaurants a surprising nonchalance on the part of the patrons about their personal belongings. One day we walked by a sidewalk café, and I saw that it was filled with businessmen. Most of them had placed on the table beside them their leather handbags, or large wallets. To do that in Rome, or Paris or New York would be to invite some passerby to grab the bag and run. In Turkey that is not so. The crime rate is very low, and you sense real security. I wouldn't push it too far, but the fact is that in Turkey there is a high level of dignity, self-respect, and honesty.

Some years ago we traveled in Turkey with my family. My son, Dan, and then-fiancée (and now wife), Kathy Vary, noted that I admired a large antique Turkish tray with the star and crescent moon motif. My wife and I returned home from Istanbul, but Dan and Kathy went on to Izmir and went to a shop where trays were sold. They were told by the owner that the star and crescent moon motif is old-fashioned and trays are not commonly made these days in that style. "However," said the shopkeeper, "I will be glad to have one made for you and send it to you in the States."

Dan and Kathy placed the order and paid in full. A couple of months later the tray arrived, exactly as ordered and promised. It was no surprise to us because we knew that the Turkish character is like that. There in Izmir, there is a man who was proud to be trusted and desirous of proving his worth.

From Izmir we went south to Kusadasi. The bus ride takes you past Ephesus, the Roman city which flourished for centuries and was a major cultural and religious center of the ancient world.

We arrived in Kusadasi early in November and found that the season had ended officially on November 1st. For this reason hotel rates were slashed, and we could go to the Fantasia Hotel which a travel clerk in Izmir had recommended.

Turkish people are interested in tourists

and very helpful. From the bus depot in Kusadasi we were helped to a minibus by well-wishers. This little van was built to hold eight passengers, but we were shortly joined by ten others who crowded in cheerily. A bit later we were dropped in front of the fabulous, five-star Fantasia.

From the road to the hotel was a distance of perhaps three or four hundred yards up a gentle slope. We shouldered our backpacks, which seemed heavy in the hot November sun, and we trudged up to the entrance of the grand hotel. The great doors opened automatically, and, as we entered, a bellhop dashed up.

"Sorry," he said, "I didn't hear your taxi."

The hotel was almost empty and we got a top-floor room with balcony looking out over the blue Aegean Sea, or as Homer called it, "the wine dark sea."

As we looked down from the dizzying height of our room, we saw below the huge complex of swimming pools and then farther away from the hotel, but not by much, the Aegean itself.

We swam in the lovely clear waters of the Sea and enjoyed super luxury (at a bargain price) for several days.

While there, we arranged with a travel agent in Kusadasi to tour the ruins at Ephesus. There were no crowds at the ruins, and we could stroll through the streets of this interesting old city and see clearly how advanced it had been. The two-story Library of Celsus is a tall building that is being restored gradually. The façade of this building is handsome and very ornate in the classical style.

We had always wanted to visit the theater at Ephesus, which is renowned for its remarkable acoustics. This huge ampitheater was built into the side of a hill by the Romans. Recently Joan Baez filled it with 30,000 fans for a concert on a summer evening.

Ephesus was at one time a city of 300,000 people. It had some of the finest buildings outside of Rome, and was a religious, cultural and trading center of enormous importance. Antony and Cleopatra visited the city. It was a gem of the known world.

Don't miss Ephesus! The wonders of this city are too numerous to recount. Also of great interest are the nearby Temple of Artemis and the fine museum near the city of Ephesus.

From Kusadasi we took the bus back to Izmir and then flew to Istanbul for a final night there and then to get our plane out of Turkey.

Turkey is a land of wonderful scenery, fantastic relics from other times, and a people who are talented, industrious and delightful to be with. In Turkey, you feel the warmth of welcome and mutual respect.

Turkey is a stronghold of commitment to the ideals of the Western World as to democracy, free trade and the general striving toward a better world for all. Go to Turkey and enjoy its hospitality and its wonders. I assure you, you will love it, and you will make new friends. Viva Turkey! A trip to this wonderful and friendly country will be one you will enjoy and remember forever!

EGYPT

Our visit to Egypt was encapsulated by the tour arrangement. We continue to believe that, for us, and perhaps for most tourists, a tour is the only way to do Egypt, unless you have lots of money and time, and/or you speak fluent Egyptian.

During the Gulf Crisis, the Egyptians suffered from an almost total loss of tourist business. The country was at war, and the Egyptians very correctly feared vandalism from Iraqi militants of one kind or another. Fortunately, the U.N. forces kept the world's greatest vandal busy and cowering at home, and we have not heard of any harm done to Egypt's treasures.

My article about the trip, which follows, discusses much of what we did and how we felt about it. Some addenda seem to be appropriate.

First of all, Lynn and I had never been caught up, particularly, by the "Egyptian aesthetic." That is to say, we had never sought out books on Egyptian wall decoration and so forth. All that, in small books, had always seemed like so many stick figures. We were truly astounded by the impact of what we saw.

The purity and elegance and grandeur of the Pharonic temples and tombs and decorations are unsurpassed by anything we had ever even dreamed of. Seeing these treasures was endlessly thrilling.

But don't wait! One should go now. The constant flow of tourists through the tombs is having seriously dangerous results. For one thing, the breath and perspiration of these hordes of people bring moisture into tombs that have sat dry as a bone for aeons. The Egyptians are correctly worried about this factor, and there is talk of closing some of the tombs.

Our Nile boat, a sort of floating hotel, stopped one day and we were bussed to the Valley of the Kings. We descended into several tombs. The most interesting was that of King Tut. In it you go down a long, rather steeply sloped shaft carved into the solid rock. This was originally built at just the right angle so that the sarcophagus could be slid down to its final resting place.

At the bottom, the floor of the excavation is level, and you go through several rooms to reach the final chamber. Interestingly, there is an "Indiana Jones" type of trap in one of the rooms. That is, there is a false floor through which you could fall if you were a sneak thief and did not know about the trap.

These rooms are brilliantly decorated. The last is the most colorful. Our guide explained that one reason that the decor has not lost its original brilliance is that the colors used were of the natural earth rather than being vegetable colors mixed by man. Furthermore, gold is used profusely, since it was a common and abundantly available metal. To the south of Pharonic Egypt was Nubia, and *nubia* means gold.

Since I am a compulsive counter, I noted as we climbed back out of King Tut's tomb that we had climbed one hundred and eighty-eight steps. I was pleased to note that even our highly educated guide couldn't answer my question when I asked her how many steps. But she did answer my other question.

"How did they light the interiors of these tombs when they were digging and decorating them, or for that matter, doing any kind of work in them?" I asked. Obviously any kind of fire would have smutted up the walls and perhaps killed the workers.

Her answer was quite intriguing. "They used mirrors and directed sunlight into the tombs," she said. She was very proud, and rightly so, of her university training. At that point we were in mid-November, and even then, ladies were carrying parasols to shade themselves from the intense sunlight. The Pharoahs certainly would have had enough light.

The following article ran almost exactly as it appears here in the regional Maine newspaper, *The Times Record*, of Brunswick, Maine, April 9, 1990.

Since neither Lynn nor I speak or read one word of Arabic, we felt overwhelmed by the idea of trying to get a good look at the treasures of Egypt in one short week on our own.

"Not to worry!" said Fritz Riegel, our knowledgeable travel agent. "The thing to do is to take a tour."

There are several tour outfits. One is Abercrombie and Kent. Another is Swan Tours. The one we chose is Misr Tours, the official Egyptian tour organization. This last has the advantage of being considerably cheaper than the others, and, we discovered, it is exceptionally good.

From the moment you arrive at the airport in Cairo until you are delivered back there by your Misr guide, you are in the hands of a set of Egyptian guides who handle your hotel bookings and all transfers from one place to another.

Our Cairo man picked us up at the airport and drove us directly to the Ramses Hilton, which is one of the fine hotels in the city. Our room on the 30th floor gave us a breathtaking view of the Nile River.

The following morning we were picked up by Amany Abdel El-Rehim and her driver. The lovely Amany, we learned, is a university graduate and knows the history of Pharonic Egypt very thoroughly. With her we went to see some of the most important and exciting landmarks in the Cairo area—or in the world, for that matter!

We saw the colossal recumbent statue of Ramses II at Memphis and the alabaster sphynx near it. We also saw the step pyramid of Zoser at Saqqara, which is the oldest man-made structure on earth.

Amany Abdel El-Rehim also guided us through the great complex of pyramids at Giza, and while there we entered the enormous pyramid of Cheops whose base covers 13 acres and which rises to a height of 488 feet. We entered and climbed the long, low passageway which ascends slowly to the actual tomb chamber. This is no trip for a claustrophobic!

Dominating the scene near the great pyramids is the enormous Sphynx. This great beast, with its human head, is constantly undergoing repairs. Its beard, which is now in England, is scheduled to be returned soon, we learned. The scaffolding around the beast does not diminish its grandeur.

The following day we were taken to the Cairo airport, and we flew to Luxor, once known as Thebes. At this ancient city we were met by another guide who introduced us to the temples of Karnak and Luxor, certainly the most imposing religious structures in the world.

We were overwhelmed by the magnitude and concept of the center. From one temple to another, a distance of more than three kilometers, there was originally a road lined with ram-headed sphynxes. These were not as large as the one at Giza, but they number in the hundreds. Most are still covered by Nile silt, but many have been excavated and can be seen today.

From Luxor we traveled to the Valley of the Kings where we entered some of the underground tombs of the Pharaohs. Most interesting is the tomb of King Tutankhamen, which was discovered intact and had never been robbed. The treasures of this tomb are now safe in the National Museum in Cairo, but the walls and their paintings are magnificent.

Near the entrance to the Valley of the Kings are two enormous statues known as the Colossi of Memnon. These great hulking giants guard the entrance to the Valley that once was an elegant showplace of tremendous size, but is now, on the surface, little more than a break in the sand and rocks of the desert region.

The early temples along the Nile are of pure Pharonic design. The later temples, after the Greek ascendancy, show the Greek influence very clearly. One of the later ones is the Temple at Esna, which now sits in a 30-foot-deep pit. This is how far down the excavators had to go to remove the Nile silt that had all but obscured the Temple.

The huge temple at Kom Ombo shows the Greek influence. This Temple was dedicated to the god Horus and to the Crocodile god as well. Kom Ombo is located at a point in the Nile where crocodiles used to sun themselves on the shore. The wall carvings in this temple are especially interesting, as they contain an annual calendar and many medical formulas and guides. Kom Ombo was a great healing center in Pharonic times.

Our cruise up the Nile was leisurely, and there was time for sunbathing and swimming. The days were hot in November, and the nights pleasantly cool. We swam in the pool on the upper deck and dined in a fine dining room one flight below. The Norwegian-built ship was comfortable. We would have enjoyed seeing a few life preservers here and there, but standards differ, and after all, they didn't plan to sink the ship.

Life along the Nile is apt to be quite primitive. We saw many horse- and burro-powered carts, and we even saw fields being plowed by oxen. The people are poor but warmly receptive. "Welcome to Egypt" is a phrase you are apt to hear anywhere, anytime.

Our river cruise ended at the Aswan Dam which has changed the whole life cycle of the lower Nile. No longer are there the devastating annual floods. Egypt now has control of the valley, and farmers can plant and harvest three crops per year instead of one as formerly.

Near the dam we visited the Temple of Philae, which was saved when the dam was built by being moved in 1970, stone by stone, to an island near the dam where its new setting is idyllic.

Our next jaunt was by plane to the ancient and tiny Nubian village of Abu Simbel. There we visited the great tomb of Ramses II with its entrance flanked by four 67-foot-high statues of the king seated. Near the tomb is a smaller one for his Nubian wife, Nefertari. These tombs which date from 1,300 B.C. were also moved to save them from the high water level of the new Lake Nasser, which the dam created.

Funds raised mainly in the U.S. and England made possible the gargantuan feat of sawing the tombs into thousands of blocks and moving them to the edge of the new lake. The relocated temples now stand 90 feet above their former level. The cost of the move in 1970 was 40 million dollars.

Although the trip by plane to Abu Simbel is a time-consuming addition to the entire trip, it is one of the most exciting events of a lifetime. Ramses II was a major leader. His tomb is decorated with an abundance of wall decorations that are unsurpassed in their beauty and interest. Here you see huge memorials to the warlike accomplishments of this great leader. The colors and designs are varied and in a remarkably fine state of preservation.

Our final chapter in Egypt was our last day's visit to Cairo during which we visited the National Museum, which is indeed a treasure trove. It is packed with marvelous artifacts from the history of the remarkable pharaohs who predated the Greeks and the Arabs, and who built a rich and abundant society based on the farming, fishing and trading wealth of the Nile Valley.

One evening we were "at liberty" in Cairo. We had heard of a good restaurant three and a half blocks from our hotel. We thought we would walk to it, but we gave up in the face of the non-stop, fast-paced traffic that relentlessly surged through the boulevard in front of our hotel. Egyptians use the horn instead of the brakes to handle pedestrian traffic, and we actually did not dare to cross the street. We are quite nimble ordinarily, but this night we took a cab for safety's sake.

Every guide we had was highly educated and enthusiastic, and we whisked through the various airports, buses and ferries that we had to take without a single glitch.

The final pay-off was that our guide, before he left us at the Cairo airport, made sure that we got through the gate with our luggage checked and our seat reservations confirmed.

There is no way that two Americans, innocent of the ways of this very foreign culture, unable to communicate by word or sign, and untutored in the special problems of traveling in Egypt, could possibly have done so much in so short a time without choosing a packaged tour of some kind.

Although tours such as the one we took are not inexpensive, we learned that to try to do alone what we did with guides would have been all but impossible and would have taken much more (expensive) time.

If you are going to Egypt, go on a tour!

Here we are at the pyramids in Giza. Probably there is nothing else in the world more impressive than Egypt.

The Hong Kong skyline with the Star Ferry in the foreground and the I. M. Pei Bank of China Building at the center.

DUBAI

Our flight from Cairo to Hong Kong was punctuated by a stopover in the Arab Emirate, or princedom, I guess, of Dubai. Dubai is located on the edge of the Persian Gulf, and there is an inlet, or river mouth, there called the Creek.

Our cabby from the airport chirped, "Ten bucks," when he realized he had Americans aboard, and we were whisked quickly to the Dubai Sheraton, a grand hotel in the International Anonymous Style that great cities and rich Arab Emirates feature.

Our trip from Cairo to Dubai was on Egypt Air and was blissfully uneventful. After the overnight layover in Dubai, presumably designed to milk Yankee dollars out of the air, we were able to get aboard our British Air flight to Hong Kong.

HONG KONG

Hong Kong, the fabled city-state of the Orient, turned out to be one of the most exciting spots in the world. It is a hard-driving commercial center where fortunes are made overnight, where hard work is apparent everywhere, and where glitz and glitter abound. We were fortunate especially in having hosts who know the place and are hard at work in it. With their help, we came to see the rich variety and dazzling beauty of the city.

The impact of arriving in Hong Kong is immediate and reassuring. The Hong Kong Airport is modern and clean, and so are the people you see there. The atmosphere is active and sensible. People are coming and going like 20th century people. They are meeting their friends and family, and they look purposeful and happy.

We were met by our hosts' driver, a bright young Chinese who whisked us to the awaiting B.M.W. 732i sedan. Then in great comfort we made the trip, not a long one, from the airport in Kowloon to #70 Kennedy Road, which is up the mountain behind the city of Hong Kong as you look at it from the harbor. Peter, the driver, got us to the apartment in a trice, and our hosts, Richard and Penny Post, were there to greet us.

The apartment is sensational. It is on the 33rd floor, which is the top floor, and it occupies the entire floor. You get off the elevator into a foyer where you leave your shoes. Then you enter into a large living room which must be nearly 40 feet square. The entire wall opposite you as you enter is one long window which looks out over the city and onto Kowloon. "Our bedroom" is also on this side of the building and has the same view as do the master bedroom at the other end of the apartment and one other bedroom, then occupied by Peck Kim Ung, a very nice young girl from Akron, Ohio.

On the left as you enter, and just off the living room, is the dining area with a window looking out the back of the apartment, and on the front, doors which open onto the terrace, often the place for breakfast.

There is another bedroom near the dining area, which also looks out the back side of the building, that is, to the south. From these rooms you look at the mountain itself, which rises sharply just behind 70 Kennedy Road. Because it is so steep, there are no buildings there, and you look out at the steep hill with evergreen covering. It makes being in the apartment seem like being out in the country.

Yet right across the street from No. 70 Kennedy Road there are stairs which go down the mountain and take you to Queen's Road East, a major artery, which in turn takes you quickly into the City Centre. It's a fifteen-minute walk from the apartment to Rich Post's office in the Bond Center in the heart of the business district. Coming back is made easy because there is, very near No. 70 Kennedy Road, a high-rise building called Hopewell Center. This stunner is round and tall. You enter from the bottom of the mountain at the entrance on Queen's Road East and take the escalator up to the first floor. From there you take the elevator to the 17th floor and then when you emerge from the building you are almost next door to No. 70 on Kennedy Road. It's magic.

Penny has done wonders in furnishing the place. The furniture is heavy and beautiful, with a lot of handsome pieces of dark mahogany. The rugs are Oriental or Chinese and go well on the beautiful highly-polished wood parquet floors. There are many Oriental touches in the decor, and the entire effect is striking and warm and welcoming. When Rich started out here, his boss told him that he must have a car and a driver. The car had to be either German or English. That meant it had to be either a B.M.W. or an M.B. or a Rolls or a Bentley or a Daimler or a Jaguar. Business people driving a Japanese car would be shooting themselves in the foot. Others would assume that the business has suffered a setback or is in some way in trouble. Hong Kong is all about making money and showing it. Never mind the fact that the Toyota Crown or the Accura Legend may be better cars at a much better price.

In Hong Kong laissez faire is the rule. Taxes are simple. You pay 15 percent income tax, and that is due the November after the year in which you made the money. Other taxes are minimal, and large projects are commonly financed by private investors. For example, the long under-the-harbor tunnel connecting Hong Kong City with Kowloon and the mainland was built by private investors. Those who got in on it have become rich. The tunnel paid out in a short few years, and continues to run at a profit. It is clean and clear and well lit. It has a freshness about it that makes it one of the best. The new East Harbor tunnel, only recently opened, also has this air of freshness.

The only gambling allowed in Hong Kong is at the racetrack, which is owned and operated by The Royal Hong Kong Jockey Club. This club works closely with the territorial government and undertakes civic projects of staggering proportions.

We visited the new campus site of The Hong Kong University of Science and Technology. This new facility will have 10,000 students when it gets going and will have cost one billion U.S. dollars to build. On Sunday the four of us drove out to the Sai Kung area to look over the site. The entire construction tab will be covered by the Jockey Club, so Rich, as a member of the club and also a member of a key committee overseeing the construction, got us into the guarded area with ease.

The campus is under construction, and the pace is rapid out there. Even though it was Sunday, the place was buzzing with activity, and there were workmen everywhere. Completion guarantees are part of the bidding arrangements, and therefore contractors want to keep as far ahead as possible so that future rain days will not hurt their profit margins.

The site is incredible. It is high on a mountain top and follows the slope right down to the sea. The scenery in every direction is breathtaking. The campus will include dormitories and faculty housing and a mansion for the President and all kinds of other ancillary buildings and complexes.

Once built, the campus will have an internal bus system and many escalators and elevators. These will be necessary because no one could make it up and down that mountain very often, if even once, in a day. Right now the rock base of the mountain is being cut away and ditched and restructured to provide for the underground conduits that will be needed for the buildings that will emerge soon.

We went to the location of the President's house. It will be on a ridge that looks out over the campus and the sea from a very great height. Behind it are three waterfalls, the largest may fall 5 or 6 hundred feet straight down the mountain side. Hong Kong wants to assert its leadership in industry and technical matters, and hence the need for this institution which is expected to draw students from all over the Orient. The new dorms will be ten and even up to 30 stories high.

We went from the Sai Kung area to Shek O, a beach and harbor section. There were people on the beach, but it was not crowded—few bathing suits and no swimmers because of the chilly air. But the water was warm. As Penny said, "Beach people are the same the world over," and it's true. There was a nice relaxed atmosphere about the place. We walked on the beach and into the ritzy housing area on the point nearby. I was reminded of the point at the tip of Bailey Island in Maine. But they are really quite different, and as you look out from where we were, there was another farther point topped by a small Buddhist shrine.

We wandered through a cluster of simple houses having an air of persistent gentrification, and we came to the windsurfer's beach. A lovely little cove with a fine sandy beach. But trashed so thoroughly that you couldn't get your feet to touch the sand on account of the coverage of plastic and bottles and a multitude of other flotsam and jetsam. Yuck! We wondered to each other why someone didn't do something about it. If a group went to work, they could clean it in a half day with no strain, it would seem. Ah, well.

We went on by car to the harbor where Rich left us so that he could park the car, and we went and got a table at a seafood restaurant called San Shui. We were on the esplanade right at the edge of the very busy harbor. Sampan taxis came and went like bees buzzing around a rose bush. A few of the boats were propelled by someone, usually an older woman, standing at the poop and working a long sweep. Most have tough little diesel engines chugging away and stinking the way diesels do, internationally. (I deeply hope that the great high tech discovery awaiting boaters will be the invention of the steam engine. It will heat its boiler with a simple, stink-free, propane-fired burner, and the quiet of the little guy will make you wonder!)

Our lunch was special. Great seafood cooked to order and consumed with that great Chinese beer, Tsing Tao (made, of course, by Germans). We ate in leisurely fashion.

After lunch we walked along the quay and looked over the busy fish market. Everyone works or watches. Everyone is busy. Old women, young kids, booted men—all are working to take care of the fish and to prepare them.

After lunch, and after our stroll along the quay, we went to the parking lot and got the Beemer, and set out to look over more of the new territories. Much is going on in the section. The Posts commented that huge housing units, 25 or 30 stories high, which loomed in certain areas, were not there the last time they had come this way. Mushroom growth. All part of the fact that the building boom in Hong Kong seems to be going on everywhere. Hong Kong has one of the largest public housing programs in the world.

Hong Kong is laissez faire, and official policies are dedicated to the proposition that what's good for business is good for Hong Kong. They don't do things that get in the way of good business success. So, there is no minimum wage. Wage levels are regulated by demand, which varies. So workers are bad off? No, the fact is that employment is high and workers are motivated because they get to keep most of what they make.

Businessmen are also motivated in the same way. Making money is a good thing, and something to be proud of. You don't have to hide the fact that you are making a good thing of it. You display your success. The signals are clear and unsubtle. For example, don't stop with the right car. Go for the gold Rolex, yuppie banner par excellence.

In Hong Kong you don't build a building these days unless you can get your money back in four years' time. So that is going to make for some interesting new developments shortly as the day of transfer of title for Hong Kong to the mainland gets closer. But in 1989 you could still do it.

How? Well, first of all you pre-sell all your space. Also you build raw space and sell it and let the new tenant finish it the way he wants to. You get in and out fast and take your winnings. There is also the art of the so-called "soft opening." This device permits you to throw up the building and complete certain floors fast and get them occupied. For example, you might get stores into the ground level paying rent and then do up the top two or three floors and sell the apartments to tenants who move right in. You see this all over the city. The apartment dweller has to step over all manner of open conduits, wire clusters, unfinished plumbing, etc., but he's in and has his new apartment and good address.

In Hong Kong you can't buy land. You lease it. New ritzy high-rise units are put up on leased land that either was not used before or was leased for much less. This creates large amounts of new income for the government, and helps to explain why it operates without any deficit. Typically this surplus, or a significant part of it, is put into building high-rise housing units which are public and available at low rents for those needing same. Also, after passing a means test, citizens can get financial help from the government to make renting a possibility.

In Hong Kong you see very few homeless bag ladies. I've seen some, but they all seem to be mentally simple, and perhaps are helped in ways that are not obvious. But there are very few. There are also practically no beggars. One person told me that the Chinese do not like to give to beggars. They feel if the guy needs money, he should go to work and earn it. I asked, "Would that be possible?" and was assured that most people could find something to do to earn at least something if they tried.

You also do not see graffiti, nor do you have your ears assaulted by cranked-up boomboxes on the streets. The explanation, I was told, was that the Chinese are repulsed by the idea of attracting attention to themselves (in a negative way, I guess, or otherwise the yuppies would turn their cuffs down over the gold Rolexes).

And you do become aware of great self-respect among these people. For one thing, they are clean and nicely dressed. I don't mean they all wear coats and ties, but a lot do. And many restaurants have brass placards saying coats required for dinner. As you walk along the street, you see people who are busy and intent upon their purpose. They are cheerful, and they look good. They dress as if they care. And they are clean. Their hair looks good. Their grooming in general is excellent. It's nice to see people who have washed their hair and brushed their teeth and put on clean clothes today. Hurray for them!

The public transportation system in Hong Kong is as good as I have ever seen, and in total contrast to the horrors of same in Istanbul or Cairo. Here there are cheery little trolleys on the main arteries busily and efficiently carrying double-decker loads of passengers. These trolleys are decorated completely on the outside, since the entire car is sold for advertising space. This has led to a city-wide art directors' competition which results in very colorful and imaginative treatment.

There are three bus companies, and their big buses are clean and modern looking. There are also 16-passenger Public Light Buses which fill in. Cabs are mostly Toyota diesel cars equipped with radio contact with "somewhere," and all reasonably new and clean and quite cheap to use. During rush hours the ride situation is helped immeasurably by the fact that British queuing holds sway. You get in line and get transportation in an orderly way.

The subway system is quite new and sparkling clean. The beautiful British-built cars have glistening stainless steel seats. Quiet, fast and easy to use. It is perhaps the best subway system in the world!

The British cars have no doors between them. On a straightaway you can look down the whole length of the train. It is a wonderful system. All New York subway system personnel should be sent to Hong Kong to see what they ought to emulate. I will contribute a dollar to that program whenever asked.

Of course, the most exciting public carriers are the ferries. The Star Ferries leave from City Centre every few minutes and take you over to Taim Sha Tsui in Kowloon. The trip costs a dollar H.K. (15¢ U.S.) and gives you great views of the city and the harbor. One ferry took us to the island of Cheung Chau, which is almost an hour's ride. The trip is sensational! You leave the city harbor, filled with boats and bustle, and then you go on past many little mountainous islands, some of which are unoccupied because of not having water.

Finally, you come to the harbor of Cheung Chau. There you stroll along the quay, which is very long and crowded at some points with markets and fish mongers. Other areas are quiet and have quay-side restaurants with café tables set out for waterside supping and sipping.

Thanks to the Posts' tireless help and skilled guidance, we saw all kinds of Hong Kong. We got to the mountain tops and into the City Centre. We saw the corporate world, and we saw little villages out in the country (which is fast filling up) with farms and duck ponds filled with tomorrow's dinners. We saw the new and we saw the old. Huge contrasts in architecture.

We also saw a variety of restaurants and had some fabulous meals. In some ways, the most interesting was The New American Restaurant in the

Wan Chai district, which features Peking Cooking. This restaurant, which has a singularly unprepossessing appearance both outside and in, is a favorite of the gourmet cognoscenti and is a favorite of Prince Charles, who goes there whenever he is in Hong Kong. We missed him on our visit, but we nevertheless had a memorable meal.

Lynn and I "discovered" The Village, which is upstairs in the City Centre. It's a rather fine place. There was only one other pair of round eyes in the place, and the service and food were tops.

Our final dinner in Hong Kong was at Jumbo, a large, really huge, floating restaurant permanently moored out in the harbor at Aberdeen. Jumbo has its own landing, and you go there and catch the ferry out to the restaurant, which is jumping with bright lights. We went up to the third floor and learned that it was filled with tourist groups, so we then went to the second floor of this palatial spread and had dinner near the throne. The throne is in almost constant use by couples who go up, are garbed in royal splendor, and then photographed either by their chums or by the professional who is equipped with a good Polaroid.

This in no half-baked operation. The throne is sumptuous in its finery, with carved, gold-leafed dragons on either side and incredible elegance and ornateness everywhere. Also, the gowns which adorn the sitters are superb. The whole scene provided us with a cheery floor show while we dined on a fine meal in the best of Chinese traditions.

We saw something of the club life of Hong Kong. On Sunday as we set off on our auto tour, we stopped at the out-of-the-city branch of the American Club. This club is located in a modern building and features a wonderful dining room, and many other club facilities including a world-class swimming pool. All views of the sea and the peaks of distant islands are magnificent. We also went to the other American Club, in the Number 2 Exchange Square Building. This, Penny informed us, is the most expensive square footage in the city, and I'm sure that means some high price! The Club is located on the 48th and 49th floors of this superb new office building. The views reminded me of my father's view from his office at 20 Broad Street. You look right out over the harbor just as he used to look out on the Lower Bay in New York. Adjectives fail, but be assured, you look and you are breathless.

We saw some of the finest hotels in Hong Kong. First off, Penny took us to a luncheon and fashion show at the Regent. We went to Kowloon by subway—one stop from the City Centre. Then we walked to the Regent and approached its grand entrance through the parking and drop-off area out front. There was an eyeful of Rolls Royces, Bentleys, sleek low Daimlers, and a very cute, bright red Opel Kadette convertible. Quite a sight!

Inside we climbed the grand staircase, which is a sight in itself, and waited outside the main ballroom until it opened. Penny is a member of the American Women's Association, sponsors of the event, and she had made reservations. We found our seats on a chart outside and were seated in great comfort just after the doors opened. During lunch the American Woman on my left, I discovered, had just recently sold a house in Westport, Connecticut. Small World!

The lunch was delicious. The fashion show was delightful and especially interesting when it came to showing new fashions in Oriental-style dresses. The ballroom itself is handsome. It is extremely elegant in a massive and yet quiet way. The ceiling is one of the most beautiful I have ever seen in a large room. Lots of gold leaf and dark mirrors. Very tasty.

After the luncheon, we walked to The Peninsula, an elegant old lady of a hotel, where tea is served every afternoon in the main lobby area. The Peninsula is old and used to be right on the waterfront of the harbor. No more. Landfill and high-rises have changed all that, and the old lady is now high and dry and far from the sea gull's scream. We got back to The Peninsula a few days later and saw the tea in operation at about 7 p.m. Very maximum high tea as only the British know how to orchestrate it. The Peninsula features restrained quietude and is a very special retreat from the hubbub of real life.

Nearby is the Hyatt Regency Hotel of international-nothing styling. Fine but anonymous. There we located the American-type bar, hidden discreetly just behind the back of a large statue of an androgynous, breasty Buddha, who I feel quite certain winked at me as we entered. Inside, we found a mix of rounds and slants and a very lovely chantoozy holding forth at a microphone and accompanied by a piano player. We idled our way through a gin and tonic while she entertained us. It was delightful

In the City Centre we lunched one day at the Furama Hotel, which we learned later has a roof-top restaurant as well as other restaurants and dining areas. We lunched in the carvery and had a pretty good meal. Not the best.

We arrived in time for the monthly meeting of Penny's gourmet group. There we were included in one of the most fantastic meals I have sunk my chompers into. Goose it was, preceded by caviar and champagne, and accompanied by an array of wondrous goodies such as would make any vegetarian into a meat eater. Penny is a great chef.

And then there was the early Thanksgiving! An incredible dinner of turkey and more fixin's than anyone ever thought possible, and a nice group of Americans to share it with. It was typical of the Posts to include others and make a meal into a feast.

Hong Kongers are proud of their skill at doing business. I took a document to a xeroxer one day. When he had done it, made the copy, I said, "Looks great. Really good." He glowed and thanked me. At the photo joint I had the following exchange. I had taken a roll of film to a 23-minute guy. He didn't quite do it in that time, but he was fast. I looked the prints over and asked for some 8 x 10 enlargements. I needed them to send off with the newspaper article I had written.

"How long?" I asked.

"One week," he said.

"No good," I said. "I need them today."

"Tomorrow," he said, cheerily.

"No good," I said. "I need them today!"

"Six p.m. " he said.

I got there at 5:45, and he had them ready! And cheap. That's the can-do attitude of Hong Kong, and they are proud of it. My photo guy was all smiles when I praised him for what he had done.

Walking in Hong Kong is a mixed activity. In the City Centre there is a system of raised walkways that is marvelous. You can go all over without descending to the street level and fighting crossovers. If you are down at street level, you benefit generally from red lights which are observed, generally, and from red and green walk lights. Of course, the fact that the British have them driving on the wrong side confuses everybody. When you walk in a crowded place, no one knows just what to do. Man's natural, God-given tendency is to keep to the right, as everyone knows. So walkers don't know what to do, and you bump into people all the time. I must say, the Chinese are very polite, and they usually apologize. They are also great about holding the elevator if you are rushing for it.

Adding to the walking confusion created by the British influence is the fact that everywhere there is construction going on. Hardly a block can be walked without stepping out into the street to avoid construction New buildings are sprouting everywhere.

The weather? In late November we hit really nice weather. From our aerie we could see the city and the other side of the harbor, always. Some mornings there was quite a lot of fog, but not to obscure the near view. We had no rain, and a mild and balmy weather pattern. But, there are ominous portents. For example, we could see that the mountainsides in the city are covered over with cement so as to direct the water flow in an inundation and guard against erosion. And then there was talk about the days when it never gets light because the rain is so heavy and continuous. Apparently July and August are only good if you enjoy living under a waterfall. So it goes.

On Sunday Rich and I went in the morning to Aberdeen Harbor to keep an appointment with a yacht salesman who turned out to be a bright young guy of the round-eyed persuasion. He whisked us into a sampan, and we went out to the junk that Rich would like to buy (or one like it). Rich feels that he could use the boat to entertain clients in a business way, and he would encourage his staff to do the same. He and Penny could also use the boat from time to time as a getaway from city, apartment life. There are, apparently, many small and almost deserted little coves which could be got to in the junk for a quiet and private overnight visit.

We looked at more than one of these junks, which are around 40 to 50 feet in length. They are unlike our yachts. Ours are apt to be designed for speed, seaworthiness and/or efficiency. The junks are designed to be good in a seaway, but spacious comfort is built into the design as well. The foredeck juts out on both sides, so that the truly boatlike prow is not visible from the deck, but there is a great deal of deck space added by this feature. Aft there is one large partly covered deck just behind the helm. These areas also feature a bar built right in to accommodate the entertaining needs of the owner.

These boats are built of heavy teak topsides and a wood called yago below the water line. They are built to last, and they are heavy. Below there will be a big six-cylinder diesel. You can easily call for a Caterpillar or a Japanese Hino. Our salesman seemed to think both are good, but the Hino is preferred because parts are cheaper and more readily available. Can't argue with that.

Some boats are on the ways and under construction right now. We explored one that will be completed in a month. It was about 52 feet in length and will cost around $100,000 U.S. Other items needed to bring the boat up to a serviceable level would add maybe 20,000 to that. Still a steal, and they can be shipped at a reasonable price to the U.S., just a few thousand. You pay for cubic footage, not weight when you ship by freighter.

I wondered about all the brightwork. These shiny mahogany elements get 4 or 5 coats of poly when new. Then each year you have the brightwork sanded and two more coats put on. That might be a heavy expense or nuisance in the States. Not so out in Hong Kong, I was assured. If you buy a junk, the way to run it is to have a man on it at all times. He's part of the boat, runs it in every way and maintains it so it's always ready to go when you are. The cost of such a man would be 5 or 6 thousand a year, so that's not a big factor. As J. P. Morgan said, "If you have to ask the cost of a yacht, don't buy one." You can see that out here in H.K. you don't have to ask, really!

Hong Kong is a huge city, but it is also a small town. People within the business and financial areas know each other. No yuppie would dream of going out in the evening in jeans and a t-shirt. He might be seen, actually probably *would* be seen. And that would tarnish his image as a suave man-about-town.

Hong Kong seems to be the product of the best influences of the British and the Chinese. The British have given them a stable, sensible government and system of jurisprudence. The Chinese, released from their natural gang and family control tendencies by this influence, have been able to work hard at business for which they have great talent. They drive hard bargains, but, as I was told, the city itself is a great proof of what they can do and of their ability to keep agreements and do good work.

It seems to me that Hong Kong should make its own way from now on. Colonialism is over, the British rule is coming to an end just at the time when that kind of thing, all over the world, is ending. The British will end it gracefully if they are allowed to. But for Hong Kong then to be taken over by the mainland Chinese makes no sense at all. Hong Kong should have its own independence, and like Andorra, Monaco, Switzerland and others, it should govern itself and keep good but somewhat distant relations with outside powers like the British, the Chinese and the U.S.

Once again, we left Hong Kong in that best of all possible ways, wishing we could stay longer and deeply appreciative of the fabulous hospitality we had received.

BALI

We flew from Hong Kong to Bali on Garuda Indonesian Airlines. Garuda is the Indonesian word for eagle, and the eagle is an important symbol there, even as it is in our country. A good name for an airline. The flight was first class in every way. Java, the largest island in Indonesia, is about 90% Muslim, whereas Bali, a very small island with under three million population, is 95% Hindu. The legend is that Bali was first populated by Hindu Javanese kingdoms who fled before the overwhelming influence of Islam. Despite the fact that Indonesia is a Muslim country, we were offered drinks before our meal. We ordered two vodka and 7-Ups and enjoyed them

Later a hostess came by and asked if we would like another. We accepted this offer.

"What would you like to have?" she asked.

"Vodka and 7-Up," I replied. Their English is excellent

A few moments later the drinks arrived, and a few moments after that we realized that I had a glassful of 7-Up and Lynn had a glassful of straight vodka!

There's a moral to that tale, but I can't seem to extract it.

Our flight landed in Denpasar, the capital of Bali, on time. It was late in the evening, and we were relieved to learn that the Balinese reception by immigration and customs officials was unsuspicious and friendly. We whizzed through with no problems and entered a world of enchantment such as we had not even dreamed of.

Our Bali visit was deeply shaped and influenced by two very important factors. First, we had been told of a guide who could get us behind the scenes and into unexpected and usually unvisited places, and second, we had been told of a hotel which turned out to be one of the most magical places on the face of the earth. Before leaving the U.S., we had written to both the guide and the hotel and had made our arrangements.

Our guide's name was I Wayan Budiasa. We asked him for two days of his time, and in his letter back to us, he said that he would be at the airport to meet us. He was there, and in that hot tropical evening, after our long trip from Hong Kong, we were delighted to see him and to get into his waiting, air-conditioned van headed for the hotel.

As we left the airport, Budi, as our guide is called, explained that the "I" at the beginning of his name corresponds to the "Mr." which we use. "Wayan" means that he was the first born, and Budiasa is his given name. He also explained that the large lighted areas we were passing by are shallow ponds used for the aquaculture of shrimp, or prawns, as they call them.

Budi's driver guided us easily through crowded streets and then along a fine new highway until we came to Sanur Beach, located on the east side of the southern tip of Bali, fewer than ten miles from the airport. In short order, we left the street and entered the long drive toward the beach, which ends at the reception desk of the Tandjung Sari Hotel, our haven in Paradise.

Budi left us at the hotel with the agreement that he would pick us up for touring, not the next day, but the day after. We wanted a day to get acclimatized. Shortly after we arrived, we were in our bungalow located right on the beach. Not even the air-conditioning took anything away from the charm of this highly unusual accommodation. Over the entrance door was a large carved protective goblin or eagle. The front door was tiny and ornately carved and decorated. It seemed more like the entrance to a temple than to a bedroom.

Inside in the welcome cool we found an unusual but very comfortable arrangement. Almost half the first floor was devoted to a large double bed and closet space. The rest was given over to a large tub, a separate shower, wash basin, and, separately, the toilet. The, to us, usual norms of privacy apparently do not prevail in Bali. Upstairs was another large bed with night stands and reading lights. The four walls upstairs were screened and curtained. We left the curtains drawn and the air conditioning on during our stay.

The next morning we stepped off the porch of our bungalow and onto the sand of a perfect beach. We swam in the clear warm waters and thought, unkindly, of winter in the Northeast of the U.S. After the swim, our breakfast was delivered on the head of a lovely Balinesian girl, and we sipped our strong and delicious dark coffee while watching the European- style sunbathers take up sun worshiping positions on the beach.

No doubt many people remember from old *National Geographics* that in Bali being topless is the usual condition for young girls. But times have changed, and now, our friend Budi told us, Bali girls are very shy. Toplessness is practiced almost not at all by young girls who are Balinese. Older Balinese women are unconcerned, and of course sunbathers make their own choices, according to this decision about as much importance as to that of whether or not to wear a hat.

Along Sanur Beach outrigger canoes cruise by and are drawn up on the beach when not in use. The skipper of #52, a man named Arya, got to me, and I agreed to hire him for an hour's cruise. We got aboard the dugout canoe and had a fine sail. Actually, the wind was uncertain and the water shallow, it being low tide, but the cruise was fun. Arya would hop out and push us over the sand whenever we went aground. He's a cheery man who plays in the Tanjung Sari orchestra for their dance evenings. A very talented and delightful chap.

Later we sailed with Arya again, and this time there was a full tide and a good strong wind from the west. We enjoyed getting outside the barrier reef and skimming through the water in that lovely little boat.

The Tandjung Sari Hotel is mentioned fondly by Anaïs Nin in her journals. She, too, was enchanted by the soft breezes and warm receptiveness of this enchanting place. Everywhere there are flowers and stone carvings. Some of the carvings are of mythical beasts, others of clownish figures, all are decorated daily with new flowers behind their ears or in their hair.

One night at the Tandjung Sari we signed up for a dinner and dance presentation, which turned out to be done by child dancers who were superb in their discipline and control. Bali is a land of dance, and these kids were tops. The next day, Sunday, we watched a class of these child dancers being trained in a space near the beach at Tandjung Sari.

It is valuable to have a guide in Bali. The venturesome tourist may want to drive his own motorcycle, moped or car, but be advised. If you hit a person in Bali, you go straight to jail— compulsory. Add to that the fact that you do not speak good Balinese, if any, and let's let that nightmare be forgotten. Go by tour bus, or get a guide.

Budi, our guide, is licensed by the government. He is bilingual and some years ago spent two years studying at the University of Arizona. His knowledge of Bali is impressive and broad in scope. He has recently been approached by an American publisher and asked to prepare a guidebook to Bali.

With Budi, we saw the most interesting temples, and the fine museum in Denpasar, and several other important tourist attractions. But we also got behind the scenes to visit several Balinese families, watch their meals being cooked and their ceremonies being prepared for.

In Bali, families tend to live in compounds. Each married member of the family will have his own living quarters, but typically there will be one well in the compound and one kitchen. In the country, the kitchen will be very simple, and there will be three cooking areas on top of the stove. Heat is provided by wood fire, often with the long logs being pushed in further and further as they burn.

Farm families will have a small, barn-like building, used to store rice, the staple of the diet.

In every family compound there is a temple with a shrine to Brahma, the Supreme God, and often several others, including one to the profession of the householder.

With Budi we entered several of these compounds and were welcomed in a quiet, but unreserved way. In one compound we found many women at work, weaving little baskets and making floral arrangements. These would be used as offerings to the gods. These people were preparing for two major ceremonies coming up shortly in the lives of this family.

Ceremonies mark a great many special events, often ones overlooked in our culture. For example, there is a ceremony at the time that the woman has been pregnant for three months, at the time of the birth of the child, and at the time, three months later, when the child's feet first touch the ground.

This is a moment of extreme importance to the Balinese. Until this time the child is considered still to be a part of the world before birth and therefore has the attributes of a saint. However, at the moment when its feet are, for the first time, allowed to touch the ground, the child joins the community of earthbound humans.

Another very important ceremony in everyone's life is the tooth filing ceremony. As far as I know, this is unique to Bali, but it is treated with importance, even to the extent that if it has not been done during a person's lifetime, it will be done before burial or cremation.

With Budi we went to Mas, a town known widely for its wood carvers. We went into workshops where carving was being done by skilled yet relaxed young people, seated on the floor and chatting easily with each other. We also went into a showroom where items of great complexity and beauty were displayed.

To be surrounded by art of exceptional beauty, both in the shops and the temples, showing absolutely no Christian or Western European influence was a new experience for us. Here the Garuda flies, with Shiwa on its back, clutching the serpent below, all planted on the back of a turtle, which, if it moves, will cause an earthquake. Here in Bali are ancient legends and a rich mythology that is all their own, totally free of our Western influence—as yet.

Bali is very different from anything we had ever experienced. The population is just under three million, and the island is about three thousand square miles in size. Ninety-five percent of the people are Hindus, and religion plays a strong part in all aspects of life.

On the streets one sees offerings to the gods everywhere. You walk around them because it would be rude to step over them, thus running the risk of exposing yourself indecently to them. There are forty thousand temples in Bali. In one of these we saw a two-thousand-year-old bell which they believe is the oldest brass bell in the world. No one, Budi told us, knows where it was made or how it got there. It is huge.

In the language of Bali there is no word for art or artist. In this pre-industrialized country, everyone has an art. Woodcarvers, stone cutters, weavers, dancers and so forth all work at their "art" in an unselfconscious and unaffected way. It is simply what you do.

The world of old Bali, preserved so delightfully at the Tanjung Sari Hotel, and in many other ways, is under attack. We had heard of Kuta Beach, the surfers' paradise of Bali, and we asked Budi to take us there one afternoon. The town is crowded with Anglos, mostly Australians, who are there for surfing and partying. In Kuta I saw the only piece of graffiti in all of Bali, as far as I know. It was on the side of a record store, and said, in large, runny, black letters, "Wild Tunes." Phooey!

On the beach, which is a wonderful one, there are crowds of surfers, sun worshipers and Bali ladies selling carvings and cloth and many other items. It's not unusual to see people getting massages from native ladies, or pedicures. It's quite a scene, but stay away if you seek the true, unaltered Bali.

We went to Ubud one day, high in the mountains of central Bali. We lunched at the Cahaya Dewata, a hotel perched on the side of a precipice. From the table at lunch, we could look far down into the valley below filled with rice paddies and divided at its base by the beautiful Ayung River. The Cahaya Dewata Hotel has three swimming pools and many rooms and villas for a first-class getaway vacation or sojourn.

On the beach and in other public areas, Balinese people are friendly and quick to say hello. Many are selling things such as carvings or watches or hats, but all are friendly. Budi told us that the Balinese do not have the equivalent of such phrases as "Good morning" and "How are you?" and the like. So these people are very direct, and they go for information. For example, having determined where you are from, the next question is apt to be, "How old are you?" or a friendly, "How much do you weigh?"

In Bali the busiest tourist month is August. December, what with the Christmas break in many parts, is also busy, but it is also the hottest month. June and July are apt to be busy, coming as they do usually right after Ramadan.

On our first trip from the airport with Budi, he informed us that we had arrived just at the start of the rainy season. But we were blessed with fine, hot and clear weather during the entire week that we were there.

Sanur Beach, where the Tandjung Sari Hotel is located, is a long beach facing out to the Indian Ocean with a fine view of Nusa Penida Islands and mountains in the distance. At one end of this beach is the Hotel Bali Beach, a high-rise looking very out of place. It is the highest building in Bali. At the other end of the beach is the Bali Hyatt, a fairly new five-star hotel styled to suggest truly Balinese design and architecture.

Tandjung Sari, which means "Cape of Flowers," is located about in the middle of Sanur Beach, which has many, many hotels. We loved Bali because in so many ways it is still charming in its unchanged old ways, and yet it is fully up to date in terms of comfort and sophistication.

We made our stop in Bali mainly because Penny and Rich Post had urged us not to miss the country. Once again, good luck and good advice, which traveled with us all the way, were right at our side.

The last entry in my daily journal for Bali goes like this:

Lunch at the Tandjung Sari. A leisurely afternoon writing cards and swimming from time to time. It is now 6:45 and it is dark. The loud drone of the beetles has just started, and it takes over. We do not want to leave. Therefore, tomorrow is the right time to leave....

Here you see a child dancer at the Tandjung Sari Hotel in Bali. Her dance is an act of devotion to the gods.

This replica of the H.M.S. Bounty has sailed from Sydney to Papeete. Beyond her stern quarters you see the Opera House.

AUSTRALIA

Of course there is something especially homey about being in a foreign country where the language is English, the cabs are fine Ford Fairlanes, the architecture is surprisingly like our own, and the way of life seems so familiar. With so many similarities it takes a bit of time to get to understand just what the differences are and in what ways they are important.

We learned from our talks with many Aussies that they have always considered themselves to be "nephews," in a sense, of the British and the Americans, and they are proud of their European heritage. Furthermore, they have in the past tended to isolate themselves from their Pacific surroundings in many ways.

In recent decades, however, a new spirit has developed in the country. Still respectful of old connections, Australia now works to nurture and cement new relationships with its neighbors. This is partly the result of the expansion of the Japanese trading influence, but it also arises from a new awareness of Australia's own potential as a force within the Pacific Trading Community.

Nowadays this country, which once kept itself aloof from non-white influences, has new attitudes and new official policies. These are highly visible everywhere. For example, the Japanese tourist business is actively sought by the Australians. Signs everywhere in tourist areas welcome the Japanese.

Restaurant menus are bilingual, and tourist information is printed in two languages. The Japanese love it, and they flock to tourist centers such as the large cities and the beach areas.

Australian immigration policies have changed, too, and the influx of non-European newcomers has grown in recent years. One group coming to live in Australia in large numbers are the Filipinos.

We read that thirty percent of Australians are of Irish descent and that Melbourne is the second-largest Greek city in the world!

When you deplane in the Sydney Airport, you are immediately struck by the informality of the crowds. Shorts, t-shirts and bare feet are in style. Cape Cod? Just about! We felt reassured that this would be a laid-back part of our journey, and we were right.

Although Sydney is a first-class, handsome, shiny and up-to-date city, with loads of productive types in suits and ties, and the busy rush of a major city, you still feel at ease with these friendly people.

Once again we benefited from good advice from our travel agent, and we stayed at the Travelodge in the downtown area. It was reasonable and comfortable and very convenient to the sights we wanted to see. If you want glitter, you stay at Sebel House Hotel, and consort with the movie stars. But that hotel is not downtown and convenient. Take your choice.

I hailed a cab at the airport, and the driver, who looked like a retired business executive on a golf vacation, turned out to be a pretty good guide. Coincidences are nice, and we loved hearing, in the course of getting his life story, about his daughter.

118

She, it seems, had lived in New York for some time and dated Stanley Rumbaugh, Jr. Now we had never known Stanley, Jr., but we knew his younger brother, David, very well, and we also knew his mother, Dina Merrill.

Two of the special treats that our cabbie told us not to miss were Captain Cook's Coffee Cruise and Doyle's Seafood Restaurant in Watson's Bay.

You get onto the Coffee Cruise at one of the central docks near the Travelodge. It's a large ferry boat type of vessel, and we sat on the upper deck and enjoyed the intense sunlight. We lucked into perfect weather during our time in Australia.

Sydney Harbor is one of the world's largest and finest. It covers over fifty-six square kilometers. The cruise goes around the edges and pokes up into some of the tributary river openings and other small coves. There are many yacht clubs, and the sailing tradition is strong. There are also many beaches of which several are nude beaches, officially so designated by the government.

Alas. What looms as so devilishly important, close up, is just about not noticeable from a bit of a distance, and we would not have even seen the nudity if our guide had not pointed it out.

The Harbor is varied in its appearance. At the city there are high-rises and busy commercial docks, but some parts of the harbor are very remote, and you would never suspect you were near a city. In some places the land is high and cliffs plunge down to the water's edge. Houses are built right up the sides of these drop-offs, one just above the other, and funicular trolleys serve the residents, almost like elevators. It looks like very nice living. Many of the houses are extravagant in design, and their views must be sensational.

As you tour the harbor, you see gun emplacements, now abandoned, which were put in place, but not action, during World War II. There is also one place at which the Australians placed an anti-submarine net during the War. The Japs sent three mini-subs to see if they could get through. One got stuck in the mesh, and the two men in it shot themselves to avoid the disgrace of being captured. Another got through and actually fired a torpedo which misfired, but nevertheless killed a number of people. One, the third, may have sunk in the Harbor, and divers are even now working to try to locate it.

Everywhere you look there are ships and ferries and small boats plying the waters. Some are big ships arriving or leaving and being shoved along by tugs. We happened to be out on the cruise on a Wednesday, but nevertheless sailing yachts were everywhere.

We saw a hydrofoil rushing by several times on its ten-minute trip to Manly Beach, near the Harbor mouth. The community of Manly Beach is on a narrow spit of land, and one side faces the Harbor and the other side faces the Pacific Ocean.

A grand sight was the full-size replica of Captain Bligh's Bounty under full sail. She was built in 1979 in complete accordance with the original plans, secured from British Admiralty files. She is 42 meters in length (approximately 120 feet), and she seemed awfully small.

This Bounty has sailed from Sydney to Tahiti, so she's no slouch in a sea way. The two concessions to modernity seem justified. She's completely air-conditioned below decks, and she's equipped with a large diesel engine. You go out on her for a day sail, and watch the crew work the ship in traditional fashion, singing the old chanties and wearing period costumes.

The Sydney Opera House is special. You can, of course, go to a show in it, or you can take a tour. While we were there, one theatre (there are four in the house) was featuring A. R. Gurney's "The Cocktail Hour." We had seen it, so we opted for the tour. This was a good choice anyway, because on the tour you get to see all four theatres, and you get an interesting lecture on the history of the place.

The story is that a competition was held, with entrants from all over the world, to select the architect for the new opera house. He would then design the building and supervise its construction.

A Dane was chosen, and work started. However, just as the exterior of the building was near completion, a new government was voted into office. New supervisors appeared, and the Dane did not hit it off with them. After many disagreements, the distraught Dane, in a fit of pique, swooped up the plans for the interior and caught the first plane back to Copenhagen.

New architects were brought in to prepare new designs for the interior, and the building was finished forthwith—not for the original estimated seven million, but for over one hundred and fifty million! What to do? Well, the wily Aussies instituted a new national lottery, and within two or three years the whole shebang was paid for.

The Opera House is, it seemed to us, an extremely successful building. It is striking in appearance, and it sits there as an important part of any view of the shoreline from the Harbor. We also were given to understand that the acoustics are wonderful in all the theatres.

The largest theatre space was to have been equipped with a revolving stage and other special features especially intended for operas. But as it worked out, the big theatre is used only as a concert hall, and operas are usually staged in a smaller space.

Dominating the city's skyline is the Sydney Tower. It shoots up one thousand feet and is the tallest building in the Southern Hemisphere. There is a two- or three-story section at the base which houses offices and shops, and then the tower rises with nothing in it but Otis elevators. At the top there is a large round area with windows all around affording great views of the city and the Harbor, a few gift shops, a lunch counter, and a small theatre. Like the Empire State Building or the World Trade Center in New York, the Tower is something you *must* do, and you are glad you did.

Our cabby-guide had recommended Doyle's Seafood Restaurant, and we had seen the place as we went by Watson's Bay on our Coffee Cruise. One day we hopped the restaurant's own water taxi and went to try the seafood.

Now the Aussies are wonderful people, but do not ever put one of them at the helm of a small skiff powered by two 200-horsepower Yamaha outboard motors. That's the mistake Mr. Doyle made, and we suffered from it.

The speed attained by the mad driver had all the girls giggling and squealing in the boat, but when we crossed the wake of a large ship, we suffered. I mean this was a bone cruncher. Giggles turned to pleas for mercy, but they did no good because the driver was isolated up forward, and the roar of the two powerplants permitted no communication.

Wrung out, and beaten to a pulp, we staggered off the dock to try Doyle's remedies. (They are about like ours here.) The food was excellent, and the bartender, on hearing our telltale accents, allowed as how he was from the States, too.

Australia is very careful not to allow people into the country on tourist and student visas unless they have their ticket of return. They do not want hippies descending on them from all over and then becoming dependents of one kind or another. Tourists are therefore generally not allowed to work. But enforcement of this restriction is casual, and in the good times the economy was enjoying while we were there, in late 1989, foreign workers were not harassed. Our waitress was a Dutch girl, also illegally but happily working.

Doyle's is indeed a good restaurant. It is attractive, the service was good, and the food was excellent. The restaurant is situated on a pier, and you can sit inside or out. We sat out and enjoyed the rural views of the little bay, one more place in huge Sydney Harbor where you are pleasantly unaware of being close to a big city.

If you like roller coasters, the boat ride to Doyle's is fine. If you worry about your health, maybe there's a bus that will take you there.

Sydney is a beautiful city. It is very modern and remarkably clean. You feel safe on the streets, night and day, and there are fine shops and good restaurants all over town.

We flew from Sydney to Brisbane and got there just for the start of Australian summer, which as they reckon it, begins on December 1.

The Aussies take sun protection seriously. This man will spray you for a dollar. You'd better do it!

Our camper was bigger than we needed, but it was extemely comfortable. We became converts to camping in New Zealand.

THE GOLD COAST

Our flight from Sydney to Brisbane (rhymes with Lisbon) was a brief one in a 747 headed on for Tokyo. Once again, we were glad that we were carrying our only luggage right with us and did not have to worry about getting things back from Tokyo.

We got our pre-arranged rented car at the airport with no delay and headed off for the Gold Coast, a seemingly endless beach to the south of Brisbane. We went to a town called Surfers Paradise.

The drive to Surfers Paradise was on a good but dull highway. It's a big town, with a cluster of high-rise buildings right at its center on the beach. We parked and walked to the sand and observed the scene.

For Australians, summer starts on December first, but on the other hand the schools had not yet closed for the Christmas break, so we were there at a good time. Many people were on the beach, but it was not jammed.

In many ways, the busy scene reminded us of a surfers' movie. Young bathing-suited types buzzed by on rented motor scooters, body builders jogged by or worked out on the beach, and supine sunbathers exposed themselves to the rays of a powerful sun.

Australians are very conscious of the dangers of ultra violet rays, and they wear a lot of sun block. Some wear colored treatments on their faces making them look a bit like the tattooed Maori natives of New Zealand. Others go to the man at the beach who has a spray machine. For one dollar he will spray your body with Coppertone from head to toe.

As we walked along, we noted the Black Whale, a second-story restaurant which looks right out over the beach and is justifiably famous. We also noted many fast-food outlets, just about like they are in America, with crowds of teeny-boppers clustered all around.

We walked along enjoying the beach, with sand on one side and high-rises on the other, and we decided that we would go on and look for a smaller town with a less miamified atmosphere.

As you go south along the Gold Coast, there is one town after another. The population of this incredible beach resort area is doubling every ten years, and the boom-town atmosphere is quite apparent. There are real estate offices on just about every street corner, and house rentals can be arranged by the week. There are also many places that rent flats by the night or week.

South of Surfers Paradise you go through Broadbeach and then come to Mermaid Beach. It was here that we found our own paradise for a week on the beach.

Mermaid Park Flats looked like an ordinary motel, but had a sign out advertising an available housekeeping flat. This unit had two good-sized bedrooms, a living room, kitchen and bath. It was clean and well equipped, and the double glass doors in our living room opened out onto a patio with a fine pool. There was a carport for our little car, and there was a washing machine. All this for

$24 U.S. per night seemed to be an impressively good deal to us.

We were exactly one block from the beach, so we could get there at least twice a day to enjoy the sunbathing, watching the surfers, watching other sun worshipers, and all those things that make a beach vacation so relaxing.

From our spot on the beach, we could look to the north and see the cluster of beach people at Broadbeach and then farther along the towers of Surfers Paradise. To the south we could see Nobby Beach and Miami and Burleigh Heads and Palm Beach North, and so on. It's all one fabulous soft, white sandy beach stretching as far as you can see in both directions.

The Australians are very beach oriented, and their life saving techniques are wonderful. At each beach there are flags in the sand to mark the limits of safe swimming, and between those flags the area is watched by ever-alert life savers, who, we were told, are a volunteer corps. They are all members of S.L.S.C., which we learned stands for Surf Life Savers Club. It's a serious and honorable calling.

At Mermaid Beach, as at the other smaller beach towns along the strip, crowding is not a problem. Around noon each day, and on weekends, the beaches are busy, but never crowded. Weekdays we took our long walks, never seeing anything even resembling a crowd. The swimming was excellent, with water temperature in the mid-seventies, and the surf, although impressive out where the surfers go, is not bad near the beach.

Mermaid Beach offers a variety of restaurants. Of course, you can go to McDonald's or to Kentucky

Fried for the usual jiffy filler when you need it, but there are also a number of other offerings. There is a good Chinese restaurant, a small Thai Café, and several Italian places, plus a pub that boasts of being the friendliest pub in Australia.

Our favorite quickly became Gino's Osteria. In this intimate and very charming restaurant, we had meals that were superb. The decor is simple, but attractive, the menu is varied, and the food wonderful, and Wendy, the English manager, knows just how to make guests feel at home.

One evening at Gino's, our very Italian young waiter, having determined that we are from New England, informed us that he was born in Sharon, Connecticut! It seems that he is a wanderer who has lived in many countries all over the world, and was then savoring the beach life of Australia.

We went to Broadbeach one evening to find out about Jupiter's Casino, a huge, high-rise hotel and gambling establishment that never closes. Yes, it's like Atlantic City, except for the fact that it is the only game in town. Buses were arriving from Surfers Paradise and from Brisbane, bringing the gamblers who yearn to run the risks and hope to take the pot.

Jupiter's is a handsome place with many of the attributes of a five-star hotel. If you are a gambler, and if you are headed for the Gold Coast, don't miss this scene. It is, of course, a fully outfitted hotel. It is not located right on the beach, but to compensate for that disadvantage, Jupiter's has an elevated monorail all its own which can whisk you to the sand in less time than it takes to deal a poker hand.

Needless to say, the airfare to Australia is a major one. However, if you are headed out for anywhere near the Gold Coast of Australia, don't miss it. It is reasonable in cost, unsurpassed in the sensational quality of its beach, and a very, very friendly and warm place to spend time.

BRISBANE

Probably most tourists skip Brisbane because of moving right on to either the Gold Coast to the south or the Sunshine Coast to the north. They are missing a delightful small city, well worth a stay of several days and well worth returning to.

Brisbane is located on the banks of the meandering Brisbane River in the State of Queensland, which has license plates proclaiming it to be the "Sunshine State." It's the Florida of Australia, and palm trees and frangipani and oleander and tulip trees and abundant other flowering trees and shrubs lend great color to the scene.

We stayed at the Travelodge Hotel in downtown Brisbane. Our room was large and comfortable, and we had fine views of the city. Like Sydney, the city is spectacularly clean compared to American cities, and there is evidence of its rapid growth and commercial bustle everywhere.

A special feature of Brisbane that pleased me very much was the fact that a great deal of clearing of tired old buildings has been accomplished in the city, yet many fine old structures have been saved. These, plus quite a few shiny high-rises and a lot of remaining open spaces make the city a very attractive one to walk in.

One day we walked to the botanical gardens, a fine park at the river's edge. It's a beautiful place, but we were somewhat disappointed to see a large gaggle of skinheads clustered in a central crossway. Somehow, on a round-the-world trip, it seemed unnecessary to us to have to be reminded that this is the tag end of the twentieth century. But it is, and there they were, just as grubby and unattractive as they would have been in London or New York but perhaps somewhat less mean? Who knows?

Our river trip lasted about four and a half hours and took us upriver on a tour boat, with a cheery guide giving us bits and pieces of information all the way. The river winds along, and here and there are rowing clubs and sailboat clubs and some areas are open for water skiing.

You pass houses along much of the trip, and the locals consider all of this area to be a part of the suburbs of the city. Farther up, the river is lined with farms, and in one place there is a swamp in which giant fruit bats were sleeping high in trees. These fellows summer in this area and go farther north for the winter. They can have wingspans of up to three feet. We did not attempt to awaken them.

We went by city bus to the Lone Pine Koala Sanctuary. This private park, recently bought and now owned by a Japanese businessman, is a great treat, especially for children and for the child in all of us.

You get to feed the kangaroos and emus, and the koala bears are very cute to look at. Truly, though, they are dull little guys, and they move very slowly. We also saw iguanas and dingo dogs and wallabies and wombats, and even a Tasmanian Devil! No family of tourists should ever miss the Lone Pine Sanctuary.

Australians are very friendly. You get in the elevator at your hotel, and someone says, "G'day."

You answer, and at once they realize that they are not hearing the usual Australian twang. "Here on holiday?" comes the question, and you're off. New friends. Good advice. Hearty wellwishes.

Thus it was that we learned of Oxley's Wharf Restaurant. It's located right smack on the river, perhaps eight or ten blocks upstream from our hotel. We cabbed out and had a delightful dinner as the sunset took its toll of daylight, and artificial lights began to twinkle up and down the river.

As we dined on excellent seafood, we were passed frequently by boats large and small plying the river. With dinner we enjoyed (as they say) a really good white wine from the Hunter Valley region near Sydney where some very fine wine-growing is going on.

After dinner we chatted with the friendly bartender and asked him about walking back to the city on the bicycle path that runs along the river. He urged us to do that, and we did.

It was dark, and we were passed by only one or two bicycles, but what really struck us was the remoteness of our route, and yet its apparent safety. We felt and were safe. This was no Central Park, full of dangers. It was a safe trail in a city, even though being very lonely. And it was beautiful.

It was getting close to Christmas in Brisbane while we were there, and the barefoot, t-shirted crowds and the large decorated and lighted Christmas tree dominating Queen Street Mall offered cheery and unexpected contrasts to us northlanders.

Across the river from our side is the new Queensland Cultural Centre which includes the Queensland Art Gallery, the Queensland Museum, the State Library, the Performing Arts Complex, and a lot of restaurants, cafés and shops. It's a handsome facility, and the tour we took was exceptionally well done.

Our guide was a young person filled with excitement and information about the place. The theater particularly interested us, and we got all around in it. It's a remarkable house seating two thousand, and fully modern in its equipment. Brisbane's climate is wonderful. It's good and hot in the summer, but pleasant all year round. We were very happy to have had time to get to know Brisbane, at least a bit.

NEW ZEALAND

New Zealand had always been one of those places you know exists, you've seen pictures of, and you accept, but you also never expect to see it. Sort of like Madagascar, or Mermansk or Tierra del Fuego. In theory it would be fun to go there, but you never really thought you would.

But as we sat in The Travel Bureau in Wilton and talked with Fritz Riegel, our knowledgeable travel mentor, we began to think seriously about going to New Zealand.

Fritz told us about one client of his who sends his daughters off on trips to various places in the world from time to time.

"The only place you can hitchhike in is New Zealand," this man told his daughters. "You'll be safe there."

The South Island of New Zealand is the one you see the most pictures of, because it has the most spectacular scenery of the whole country. It has a mountain range called The Alps. It has Milford Sound on its southeast coast, and this Rudyard Kipling called the "eighth wonder of the world."

New Zealand lies two thousand miles to the east of Australia. The first settlers in Christchurch, the capital of the South Island, were all Anglicans, who had to get approval from their parish priest and then their bishop before they could emigrate to the new colony.

Dunedin, a major city located to the south of Christchurch, was settled later by Scots and is still a predominantly Scottish city. The *edin* in Dunedin has the same Celtic origin as the *edin* in Edinburgh.

Or is it the case, as some believe, that Dunedin was named after Edinburgh, and that Edinburgh is Edwin's burgh (or town)? Edwin was King of Northumbria, which in his day extended from the River Humber in England (hence Northumberland) to the Firth of Forth in Scotland. Actually, we did not worry much about these matters. We simply noted the mystery with interest.

The South Island is very rural and underpopulated by European or American standards. Once out of the small number of mostly small cities, you drive through ranchland, farmland, and parkland. The roads are good, the views are spectacular, and the traffic is very light.

Following the advice of our trusted travel agent, we had booked a hotel room at the Airport Travelodge in Christchurch before leaving on our trip. We had also arranged for renting a camper van from a rental agency called Newman's, right next door to the hotel.

First, we spent several days in Christchurch and explored this small but interesting city, which seems right out of Old England. The architecture is very English, and the bobbies wear helmets as in London. The English spoken by the Kiwis, as New Zealanders are called, seems much less strident than the Aussie version.

One day we took a city bus tour to Akaroa, a small town located over the mountains from Christchurch. It is a fishing village and was originally settled by French settlers who were lured to it by a French real estate promoter who had bought land on the edge of Akaroa Bay and wanted to sell it off.

But, when the shipful of settlers arrived, they learned that the British had filed their claim of ownership first, and the French were out.

All this confusion was worked out somehow, and we looked forward to the little touch of "French culture" we were about to visit after a sensational bus trip over the mountains.

We had been primed for a bit of France by the travel literature given out by the city bus company, and other references to the foreign atmosphere of Akaroa. So our anticipation mounted as we entered town going by a charming little inn right on the shore called *Hôtel des Pêcheurs*. Farther on, as we entered the town itself, we noted with pleasure that the streets were all named with French names. "What fun!" we told ourselves. "Un petit morçeau de la belle France, içi même!"

Wrong! The first store we went into to get a bit of ice cream was run by a squawky woman who, in answer to my query, chirped, "Oh, no, love, there aren't any French around here at all."

Akaroa is a Maori word meaning *long bay*, and we took the tourist boatride out to its end. It was a very beautiful trip, and we saw Hector dolphins, which are not to be seen everywhere, and got an idea of the rugged headlands of the coast.

Back in Christchurch after our trip to Akaroa, we accepted the advice of our driver, Peter Kenner, and repaired to the Oxford Pub, a very British place crowded with late afternoon yuppies and general good cheer. There I realized that I did not have my camera, and what ensued is explained in the following letter which I wrote joyfully on my little portable typewriter later that evening.

I sent the letter to the manager of the city bus line with a copy also sent to the Editor-in-Chief of the Christchurch newspaper, *The Press.*

Re: <u>How I Learned to Love New Zealand!</u>

Dear Sir,

I will be delighted if you want to share this amazing story with your readers and thus decide to run it in your paper. But at any rate, I must share my pleasure with someone, so here goes:

Yesterday my wife and I took a bus tour trip to Akaroa. The driver, Peter, picked us up at the Travelodge at the airport, and off we went for a fabulous trip, well guided by the informative Peter, who knew and loved every turn in the road.

We got back to Cathedral Square at about 5:30 and repaired to the Oxford for a fine glass of wonderful New Zealand wine. Just as I was finishing this delicious libation, I realized that I did not have my camera. I should explain that I am a professional photographer and am here both as a vacation and to get photographs to be used in a show when I get home to the U.S. in January.

We rushed to the bus kiosk in the Square, only to find that it had closed at 6 p.m. Then my wife noticed a light, and we knocked, and a small window opened. I explained my problem to the very intelligent and concerned young man who was at the window, and he said that he would ring up the garage and see if the camera was still on the seat of the bus. We waited just a few moments, and the call came back from the garage—The Camera Was There!

I offered to hop into a cab and go to the garage, but the man who had found the camera said he would be right up to the Square with it. True to his word, the man arrived a few minutes later and approached me with the camera and a coin.

"What's that?" I asked, pointing to the 20-cent piece.

"It was on the seat with the camera," he said, smiling broadly.

I pressed a bill into the hands of this angel of merciful honesty, and thanked him with all my heart. He was happy to have done a good deed, my wife was relieved beyond words, since she had dreaded living with me cameraless for the rest of our trip, and I was overcome with appreciation for the fine spirit of New Zealand good-heartedness. The despatcher came out and said with a great smile that he hoped we would enjoy the rest of our stay in New Zealand.

Enjoy it! I will never forget the smile on the face of this nice guy who handed me my state-of-the-art, fully computerized, $750 U.S. camera *and* my twenty-cent piece!

Lynn and I were not at all sure about Fritz Riegel's advice to rent a camper van in New Zealand.

We'd never done any camper, or even camping, tourist trips in the States, and we had a lot of questions.

But a-camping we did go, and it was an idyllic time. Our Newman's Kamper, all arranged for from Wilton, Connecticut, before we left, was a biggy. It had bunks enough for six, a nice dining and sitting area in the stern when the bed was not made up, a kitchen, a bathroom and a fridge. The whole unit was built onto a Daihatsu truck chassis, and the powerful diesel six was up to everything except comfortable high speeds.

In New Zealand every town has at least one campground, and some campgrounds are located out in the country. All are equipped with a kitchen, a common room, washrooms, and often they have laundry machines as well. Even the most simple campgrounds are nicely maintained and fresh and pleasant to use.

At campgrounds you can "plug into the mains," which means to use their hook-ups. Generally we used their electricity, but we used the public washrooms in preference to our own somewhat cramped bathroom.

In one campground, we noticed a very small tent next to us. In the morning two Dutch girls emerged from the tent. They used the communal kitchen for their breakfast, and we learned that they were in New Zealand looking for work on an organic farm. We gave them a ride to the next city on our way.

Driving the big Daihatsu truck was exciting. I was slow in developing an accurate sense of distance on the left side, and many a shrub, tree and fence is a bit different now from what it was before we drove by. Actually, when we picked up the camper and inspected it with the agent, I noted bruises all over the left side of the van, and he said not to worry about them. Apparently many Americans and Europeans who rent campers have difficulty judging their distance from things on the left.

Why these good folk, and the Australians and the Irish, too, do not convert to driving on the proper side of the road I do not know. There should be a standard, all over the world, and obviously, it should conform to American usage.

The drive to Milford Sound is a must. You cross a kind of continental divide which is part of the spine of the South Island. At that high spot we got out and fed crumbs to the wild parrots, while chatting with trekkers who had hiked from the Sound's edge up to this place. The hike, called the Milford Trek, is a three-day one and is about thirty miles long over tough mountainous territory.

From the divide, we entered the mile-long Homer Tunnel, which is quite new and saves many miles of steep and winding roads. The tunnel has a two-lane dirt road in it and is inadequately lit. After the tunnel, you descend to the water's edge over many miles of winding, narrow roads.

Coming around one corner, I met a huge Volvo bus coming at me at high speed and well over the line into my lane. I did not have time to look around, and I had to pull to the left and fast. I avoided the impending head-on collision quite well, but I also wiped out a large traffic sign explaining that there were dangerous washouts ahead. This also took out my left rearview mirror.

At the time that we took this drive, there had recently been heavy rains so severe that the lodge at the Sound had closed, and evacuation plans were made to get the few residents out of the service area. The result was that all around us, in the towering mountain sides, there were literally thousands of tiny waterfalls carrying the runoff from the storm. It seems that in this rugged terrain there is very little topsoil, and every rainstorm creates waterfalls.

The lodge and campground at the water's edge reminded us of Breckenridge, Colorado. It's a woodsy place with a large, handsome, rustic living room, a huge fireplace and a large TV set. We were amused to see that the only channel they can get is CNN.

We also noted that the remoteness of the place and the high barrier of the surrounding mountains mean that I could get almost no radio reception. My little short-wave finally delivered a rasping newscast in Spanish, but I never discovered its source.

We pulled into the lodge and arranged for a spot to park the camper. Then we hunkered down, getting supper and generally relaxing. The scene in and around the lodge was a beehive of activity. Backpackers were everywhere, many treating severely damaged feet banged up on the world-renowned trek.

Milford Sound is technically not a *sound* at all. It is a fjord or narrow inlet of the sea, between steep slopes. Mitre Peak, a mountain at the water's edge, rises abruptly more than five thousand feet above sea level, and the depth of the water is more than fifteen hundred feet. On one trip, we were told, the *Q.E. II* came into the Sound, but she could not stay overnight because they could not anchor in water that deep.

We walked on a footpath to Lady Bowen Falls, a sensational five-hundred-foot waterfall near the lodge. Then we took a fine tour boatride out to the end of the Sound, at which point the Sound narrows to only about six hundred feet in width. The boat was filled with tourists from many places, although no Japanese. We figured that the Japanese, who have come to love Australia, probably find the Scottish-like climate of New Zealand not very appealing.

Milford Sound is a truly magnificent place. It is remote and thankfully unspoiled, and the few who are lucky enough to get there obviously enjoy it the way a great park should be enjoyed.

On our return trip, we stopped once again at the continental divide, this time to pick up a pretty young hitchhiker. Helen, her name, is from London, and she had just completed the trek and needed a ride to help on her way back to Christchurch.

We asked her about hitchhiking, and she said that she hadn't done much of it, but she felt quite safe, seeing us doddering along in our camper. "There are very few killer camper couples," she said.

When Helen heard that we were headed for Queenstown, she told us about The Stonewall Café. "This is the best place in town to eat," she advised. We dropped Helen off at the crossroads in Lunsden, and headed north to Queenstown, up a long, lovely and meandering valley.

You have the Mataura River on your left most of the way, and the country is remote farming and ranching territory. Around one corner, we came upon a sheep herd, all over the highway. The sheepherders waved at us to come on, and we slowly knife-edged our way through the milling crowd.

Closer to Queenstown we drove along the shore of Lake Wakatipu. This is very remote country. We saw one fisherman at the shore and one small commercial fishing boat out in the lake, otherwise, no one for miles and miles.

Queenstown is at about two thousand feet, and in the winter it is a ski resort. We were there in mid-summer, but it was chilly. I asked a chap in line at the post office one morning, "When does the ski season start?"

"Tomorrow," he said, "if this weather keeps up."

Queenstown is right on the edge of Lake Wakatipu, and it is surrounded by mountains that resemble the Scottish highlands. A handsome backdrop in the distance is provided by a chain of mountains called The Remarkables, which were snow-covered on our first morning in town.

Lake Wakatipu is over fifty miles long, and the mountains rise right from its shores. To get out on the lake, you can take the excursion steamer, the *Earnslaw*.

The *Earnslaw*, named after the towering mountain peak at the north end of the lake, is a great character boat. She was built in New Zealand in 1911 (the same year as the Titanic!) and brought in sections up to Lake Wakatipu by railroad. She was assembled at the edge of the lake and then launched.

In 1911 in New Zealand they had to take what they could get when it came to putting a power plant in the *Earnslaw*, and what they could get were two steam engines built for railroad use. They are still in service in the ship, and they are fueled with hand-shoveled coal. They burn a ton an hour when she's doing her thirteen knots out on the lake. From the upper deck one looks down on the men working hard to keep the fires fueled.

The *Earnslaw* is one hundred and sixty feet long with a beam of twenty-four feet. She is kept as spic and span as she was the day she was launched, and you sense the pride of the captain and the crew at all times.

We noted this attitude especially when a child locked herself in the ladies' and had a screaming fit. The door had to be broken open with a crowbar, but most of us seemed to be hoping that no irreparable damage would occur. The child and the boat survived somehow, and we all went back to singing "Waltzing Matilda" and other songs as led by a piano player on the after deck.

The *Earnslaw* excursion took us across the lake to a sheep station or large ranch, huddled on the narrow coastline. Here they graze twenty-five thousand sheep and two thousand head of cattle. We watched the incredible partnership of man and dog as a crowd of sheep were expertly nudged into a corral and readied for shearing.

Our host-guide at the ranch explained that in mountainous country like this, handling sheep on foot or on horseback would be impossible. The dogs are essential to the work.

"If a disease wiped out our dogs, New Zealand would be out of the sheep business overnight," said our swag man.

Sheep are strange animals. They have little fighting blood, if any, and once turned over on their backs, they submit to the indignities of the shearing without a trace of struggle, much easier than giving a five-year-old boy a haircut, I recalled.

Queenstown is a small and simple mountain town. There is a good old-car museum and many good, very old, American cars still in service. We took a cable car to the top of a mountain overlooking the town and the lake and had dinner at the top in the good restaurant located there and watched one after another hang glider soar out over us and gradually ride the currents down to the athletic field right next to our campground.

The Stonewall Café was reasonable and first class. It has a friendly atmosphere and the food was superb. Our lamb chop orders included six (!) chops each and cost only about eight dollars American. There was a two-dollar corking fee for the bottle of good New Zealand wine that we brought with us, thereby observing their B.Y.O.B. regulations. We loved the place and regretted that we had not gotten Helen's address in London so that we could thank our hitchhiking friend for the tip.

In New Zealand we became converts to camping. We never had to worry about reservations, and the cost of a spot in a campground is very small and always well under ten dollars U.S. We met interesting types and we savored that nice feeling that comes with beating the system.

Back in Christchurch we turned in our camper, shouldered our backpacks, and hiked to the airport for our flight out. We left feeling that New Zealand would definitely be high on our list of places to return to, if ever we get a chance.

TAHITI

If I were one and twenty, and wanted to be a businessman and become rich fast, I would avoid M.B.A. programs, of course, and I would relocate to one of three places: Russia, Australia or Tahiti. Russia would be the least attractive because of the bureaucrats who won't be out of the way for a long time. Australia would be delightful because it is such a friendly place and so underpopulated. Tahiti, and specifically the city of Papeete, would be my first choice because it is small, bustling, and has a certain Gallic *je ne sais quoi*, which we found to be intriguing.

Tahiti sits out there in the middle of the Pacific, about equidistant from Sydney, Australia, and L.A. It is the port city for all the Society Islands, and all merchandise goes through Papeete, both incoming and outgoing. Papeete will grow most certainly as growth occurs in the Islands. And life there could be very pleasant.

For example, in Tahiti you are away from the rest of the world by thousands of miles, and yet you are in a vital trading center. If you judge things by automobile brands, you will find that even here in French Polynesia there are more B.M.W.'s than you've ever seen. Of course, the French sell their cars and trucks in this captive market, but there are many who can afford the truly unnecessary showpiece that a Beemer is.

Papeete is a rich commercial city. There are good restaurants—we especially enjoyed Acajou, located right on the waterfront. Fritz had told us about its unusually fine Chinese menu. There are some downtown hotels. We stayed at the Prince Hinoi, a rather standard commercial hotel, for eighty dollars a night. We were comfortable.

When you walk along the quai, you pass a long row of incredibly grungy yacht-type boats, tethered to the stone walkway and tied to buoys out in the water. Many of these look abandoned. It's quite a dismal scene.

However, at night there is one area where the trucks roll in, and each opens out to reveal a restaurant of some kind or other. The possibilities included French, Chinese, Mexican and an array of others. This was the way to get a cheap and very good dinner in Papeete.

The open market, housed in a huge municipal building, is something like what Les Halles used to be in Paris. There are stalls selling all kinds of foods and clothing and souvenirs and flowers and fresh fish, and on and on. Outside there are pigs tied, apparently awaiting the butcher's knife. The scene is busy, noisy and very colorful. Not to be missed.

Downtown Papeete bustles, during both daytime and nighttime, and it was very interesting to us. Architecturally, it's a mess. Dull buildings abound, and there are no views that are visually satisfying in the city. However, there is the energy, and back up in the hills there are homes that would make a fine place to live. Up there one gets sensational views of the harbor and the city, and, of course, the broad Pacific.

Papeete does not rate very high on most tourists' lists. A quick survey covers most of the local color, and then off they go to a resort hotel, and there are a lot of them located just outside of the city. The problem is that once in those hotels, you could be in any warm-climate resort in the world. The crowd might be a bit more international, and the French cuisine a bit better here, but in other ways it could be Hawaii or Mexico or a West Indian island. Nice, but predictable.

We took the tour around the island and saw Venus Beach. It's the only good beach of any size on Tahiti. The sand is volcanic black, and as on all French beaches the amount of sunburning going on is noticeably more than on an American beach.

We got to the Gauguin Museum, which badly needs help from some of those money-making tycoons of Papeete. They have assembled a lot of stuff related to the great man's career in this museum, such as large blow-ups of newspaper articles about him, and photographs of the old days. Since they have only three small and unexciting examples of his work, the museum is not a mind-blower. Two of these are on loan.

It was interesting to see this little museum, but it's a long ride out, and there is not much there, really. Gauguin loved the islands, but as soon as he died the zealots destroyed his erotic art and artifacts, even including decorated buildings, so the memory lingers on, but the memorabilia are scarce.

Fortunately, we are all familiar with the paintings he did of charming Polynesian nymphs, proudly arrayed in their colorful cloth wraps, freshly shipped in from Paris and all the rage.

We went to a hotel on Bora Bora, which is a long trip by plane from Papeete, and then by ferry and then by bus. The hotel was elegant and very expensive. We had felt that we should, somehow, see how it's done out there, and it's done very comfortably, for sure. But even here the beach is not really good. There's a barrier coral reef, so you are safe from sharks, but there's also a lot of unpleasant coral all around, and you wade carefully out for a long time before you get to good swimming depth.

The sand is nice, and the views are lovely. If you enjoy exploring just to learn about how people do their expensive vacations, don't miss Bora Bora. But don't go there looking for excitement, sensational beaches, or glimpses into a truly foreign and different culture. Stay in Papeete for that.

From Bora Bora we flew to Moorea, another of the hotel-oriented islands near Tahiti. It is picture-book lovely, with great mountains rising mightily from the bright blue sea (play music from "South Pacific" on your Sony Walkman). We took the tour bus around the island and saw the famous (or they ought to be) chickens that fly. Our guide, Angelina, was very beautiful and spoke excellent English—also French, of course.

I asked Angelina how her family would feel if she were to marry a non-Polynesian, an American for example. She shuddered visibly, and allowed as how they would be very angry.

In a brief stay, one gets only hints about the relationship between the French and the Polynesians, but there are clues that are suggestive. For example, the French influence is evidenced by the existence of mail-box-like units located next to the real mail boxes. These are there to receive the morning delivery of the baguettes, or loaves of

French bread—good evidence of the civilizing effect of the French.

On the other hand, there are two police forces in Tahiti, one French and one Polynesian. Something must be signalled by that fact, but we remained blissfully unaware of what it might be.

Really surprising to a tourist like me especially after the constant harassment you get in a place like Egypt, is the fact that you are warned even by the stewardess on the airplane as you approach Tahiti, "Do not tip or offer tips!"

Accepting a tip would be undignified, and offering one would be insulting. That kind of personal dignity is easy to take, especially when everything costs at least twice what it ought to. That comment is a bit unfair, because all island countries have to import just about everything, and thus prices have to be high. This is true even in Puerto Rico. But Tahiti is exceptional.

We stopped for lunch at Le Bateau, a wonderful French restaurant out on the water, located on a guess what? Right! A boat. The food was marvelous, and the charm of the atmosphere of this great restaurant couldn't be outdone even by the finest of Hollywood crews charged with creating a truly South Pacific exile motif.

I wanted to buy a Panama hat and drape myself over the bar at Le Bateau for a few weeks and tell stories about my past as a pirate to all the tourists as they came in each day. I figured that each would set me up for a drink or two, and thus the stay would be quite cheap. Lynn said, "Walter Mitty had fun, too."

For the record, Le Bateau has rooms to rent also, and I suspect they are simple but okay, and I also suspect that if you stay there you will pay less than two hundred and fifty dollars a night as some people have to do on Moorea.

Back in Papeete we had to get up quite early to get our plane for L.A. As we emerged onto the street from the Prince Hinoi Hotel, we did not see where to get a cab, but in the cool freshness of the early morning, some of the leftover ladies of the evening wandered by. In their friendly way they helped us get a cab.

Our plane for L.A. was on time, and our reservations were in order. We got aboard, stuffed the backpacks under our seats, and prepared for the flight that would effectively bring our exotic trip to an end. It was sweet sorrow. We looked forward to being greeted by our son, Bill, in L.A., and getting home to the rest of our family in the East. But we had grown accustomed to wandering, and the final stanza was definitely orchestrated in an elegiac key.

FIN

PACKING FOR THE LONG TRIP

Packing for a long trip was a completely new challenge for us, and we asked a number of travel-wise friends for suggestions.

"Do not check bags!" said our son, Bill.

"Do not carry anything in your hands," said travel-wise Jack Aley, our environmentalist friend, who had been attacked by gypsy children in Rome while making his way to his hotel.

We decided to try to find backpacks that would go under the seat of an airplane, and after some searching, we found just the items we wanted at a large sporting goods store. Our backpacks measured less than 45 inches, that's height plus length, plus width, and that makes them legal on almost all international flights. On small local flights here and there, we did have to check our bags, but we could see them go on board, and we did not worry.

Our packs had handles so that they could be carried like regular suitcases, a shoulder strap for over-the-shoulder carrying, and regular backpacking shoulder straps and waist straps for longer distances.

What to put in these wonderful bags? Well, we packed over and over again before we left to make sure that our packing ideas were realistic. As we did this, we refined our lists so that on the day of our departure we knew exactly what to reach for and what to put in.

Our packing was complicated a bit by the fact that we would be in northern Europe for several weeks of increasingly cold fall weather. But later in the trip we would be in Bali and Australia in the heat of summer. A further complication was that we occasionally would be in rather fancy hotels and clubs in sophisticated cities like London, Paris and Hong Kong, yet we would also be staying mostly in rather simple, off-the-main-track places as well.

Our lists were as follows. Note that all items where possible were of light-weight, washable and permanent press materials, and we took care to take things that would go with each other in the color department.

<u>Lynn's List</u>

3 pairs of slacks
6 blouses or shirts
1 pair culottes
1 dark blue sweater
5 pairs underpants
3 bras
1 half slip
4 pairs stockings
2 pairs of knee-highs
2 pairs bobby socks
1 pair sneakers (worn on the plane)
1 bathing suit
1 light-weight bathrobe
1 tiny fold-up plastic raincoat
1 Burberry coat with liner
1 small cotton scarf
2 pairs shorts
1 nightie
1 rain hat
1 very small umbrella
1 large, light wool scarf
1 shower cap
1 pair dress shoes

1 pair sandals
1 pair flat leather shoes
3 dresses

Lynn also took a small amount of inexpensive jewelry made of plastic, semi-precious stones and shells, and two purses which packed flat when not in use. One was rather dressy and the other a simple daytime bag.

In the practical, laundry-management department, Lynn took two folding hangers bought at a travel store, small packets of detergent, Ivory soap, a sewing kit with scissors and safety pins, a plastic clothesline and a stopper for unequipped sinks.

<u>My List</u>

3 pairs light-weight slacks
2 dress shirts
4 pairs black socks
1 thermal underwear vest
1 windbreaker jacket of parachute cloth with
    zipper closing
1 thin plastic raincoat
1 bathing suit
2 pairs shorts
4 short-sleeved shirts
1 safari jacket
1 short sleeved wool sweater
1 very small umbrella
4 pairs underwear briefs
1 pair leather sandals
several handkerchiefs

1 pair corduroy trousers
1 small backpack for day trips
1 cotton hat with visor
Rocksport leather shoes
1 navy blue sport jacket
1 pair flip flops

Because I am a photographer, I carried one camera and packed a small back-up camera in my bag. I also packed a tripod and an extra lens for my main camera. I had bought two lead bags for carrying film, but I learned that airport X-ray does not seem to damage slow film, and I stopped worrying about that factor with no bad results.

While we were actually on long flights, we wore clothing that would be comfortable but also somewhat dressy. I always wore a shirt, tie and jacket on the theory that airport officials are apt to treat well-dressed people with a bit more respect than slobs. The tactic seemed to work well.

Without exception I wore a money belt with a zippered inside pocket. In that I kept six one-hundred-dollar bills as an emergency stash in case we were robbed. Lynn wore a small packet which attached to her bra strap for the same purpose. We never needed to use these reserves.

We both wore "fanny packs" around our waists at all times. In these we kept our tickets, credit cards (we took two of the most famous ones), passports, driver's licenses and hotel confirmations. We were never separated from these packs. They even went to the beaches with us, and stayed, wrapped in towels, under our watchful surveillance.

U.S. dollars are the international currency. In Dubai we caught a cab to our hotel, and I told the driver I had no Dubai money, and he said, "Ten bucks." No problem.

In Istanbul our host, a Turkish banker, was about to leave on a trip to Libya. He happened to open his wallet in my view, and I saw a large supply of U.S. banknotes.

We decided to keep with a goodly supply of small U.S. bills for easy settlements anywhere in the world.

Other items that we carried that proved to be invaluable were the following. We had a very tiny, high-powered flashlight; a good, not expensive, battery-powered travel alarm; and a tiny radio with AM, FM and six bands of short wave.

I was glad that I had thought to put in a large supply of business cards. We swapped these all along the way with new friends here and there. And don't forget your address book. Friends love to hear from you from exotic places.

Of course we took the toilet articles we knew we would need. A special note: be sure to take what you think you might need with you, rather than count on buying things overseas. Foreign formulations are apt to be different, even though the brand names are the same. Australian aspirins are three grains, for example, and overseas Listerine tastes totally unlike ours here in this country.

We had Xerox copies of our passports, credit cards and other important numbered items made before we left. We carried a set of these copies in in our backpacks and also left a set on our desks at home. We never had to use them, but we felt it was good insurance.

Our trip lasted three months and three weeks. One of our great pleasures as we traveled was keeping a daily journal. For this I used a standard stenographer's spiral notebook. For writing articles to go along with my photographs, I carried a lightweight old Olivetti typewriter, which worked like a charm and was no trouble to keep with me.

For safety we took extra pairs of glasses and sun glasses, and we also took eye covers for sleeping on daytime flights. Our French-style wine bottle corkscrew was invaluable on a number of occasions, and even proved its worth on the fast train from Paris to Marseilles, where the hostess herself was unable to find one in her own kit.

Small paperback novels are the best. You can always stick one in your pocket, and long trips provide ample time for catching up on your reading.

We felt lucky in that we took nothing with us that we did not use, and we did not have to buy items along the way because we were adequately supplied. Our list worked, and we were happy with our not-very-fancy backpacks. They looked as though they might be stuffed with dirty laundry, and that's a safety factor. Don't feel you have to impress the hotel clerks with your fine luggage. Play it safe and you'll be glad you did.

DATE DUE